KU-464-810

ABERDEENSHIRE
LIBRARIES

WITHDRAWN
FROM LIBRARY

ALIS
3053486

HOW NATURE WORKS

HUMAN BODY

WEB LINKED

First published in 2011 by Miles Kelly Publishing Ltd
Harding's Barn, Bardfield End Green, Thaxted, Essex, CM6 3PX, UK

Copyright © Miles Kelly Publishing Ltd 2011

10 9 8 7 6 5 4 3 2 1

Publishing Director: Belinda Gallagher
Creative Director: Jo Cowan
Design Concept: Simon Lee
Volume Design: Rocket Design
Cover Designers: Kayleigh Allen, Simon Lee
Indexer: Gill Lee
Production Manager: Elizabeth Collins
Reprographics: Stephan Davis, Jennifer Hunt,
Anthony Cambray
Consultant: Camilla de la Bedoyere

All rights reserved. No part of this publication may be reproduced, stored in a retrieval system, or transmitted by any means, electronic, mechanical, photocopying, recording or otherwise, without the prior permission of the copyright holder.

ISBN 978-1-84810-470-9

Printed in China

British Library Cataloguing-in-Publication Data
A catalogue record for this book is available from the British Library

Every effort has been made to acknowledge the source and copyright holder of each picture. Miles Kelly Publishing apologises for any unintentional errors or omissions.

MADE WITH PAPER FROM

A SUSTAINABLE FOREST

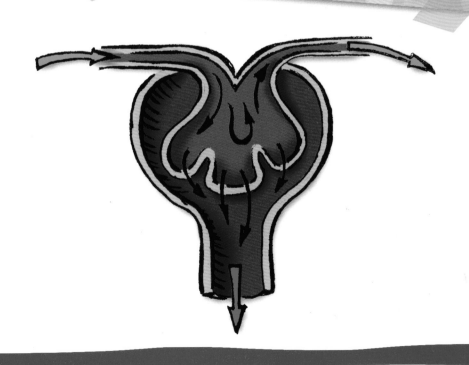

HUMAN BODY

By Steve Parker

Illustrated by Alex Pang

Miles Kelly

ACKNOWLEDGEMENTS

All panel artworks by Rocket Design

The publishers would like to thank the following sources for the use of their photographs:

Front cover: Fotolia: (c)York
Back cover: Shutterstock: (c)beerkoff

Getty Images: 32(b) MCT

Rex Features: 7(cr) Sipa Press

Shutterstock: 6(c) muzsy; 6(b) Triff; 8 Monkey Business Images; 10 Vishal Shah; 12 Taranova; 14 bezikus; 16 JonMilnes; 18 beerkoff; 20 Daniel Rajszczak; 22 paul Prescott; 24 Picsfive; 30 Remzi; 33 (br) Alex Luengo; 35 Oleinikova Olga; 36 Patricia Marroquin Science **Photo Library:** 7(b) SIU; 27 Dr P. Marazzi; 29 Simon Fraser/NCCT, Freeman Trust Newcastle-Upon-Tyne; 32 AJ Photo

All other photographs are from Miles Kelly Archives

ABERDEENSHIRE LIBRARY & INFO SERV	
3053486	
Bertrams	19/09/2011
J612	£5.99

WWW.FACTSFORPROJECTS.COM

Each top right-hand page directs you to the Internet to help you find out more. You can log on to **www.factsforprojects.com** to find free pictures, additional information, videos, fun activities and further web links. These are for your own personal use and should not be copied or distributed for any commercial or profit-related purpose.

If you do decide to use the Internet with your book, here's a list of what you'll need:
• A PC with Microsoft® Windows® XP or later versions, or a Macintosh with OS X or later, and 512Mb RAM

• A browser such as Microsoft® Internet Explorer 9, Firefox 4.X or Safari 5.X
• Connection to the Internet. Broadband connection recommended
• An account with an Internet Service Provider (ISP)
• A sound card for listening to sound files

Links won't work?
www.factsforprojects.com is regularly checked to make sure the links provide you with lots of information. Sometimes you may receive a message saying that a site is unavailable. If this happens, just try again later.

Stay safe!
When using the Internet, make sure you follow these guidelines:
• Ask a parent's or a guardian's permission before you log on.
• Never give out your personal details, such as your name, address or email.
• If a site asks you to log in or register by typing your name or email address, speak to your parent or guardian first.
• If you do receive an email from someone you don't know, tell an adult and do not reply to the message.
• Never arrange to meet anyone you have talked to on the Internet.

Miles Kelly Publishing is not responsible for the accuracy or suitability of the information on any website other than its own. We recommend that children are supervised while on the Internet and that they do not use Internet chat rooms.

www.mileskelly.net

info@mileskelly.net

CONTENTS

INTRODUCTION

The human body is perhaps the most studied object in the world. As well as being endlessly fascinating, it contains a dozen main systems that are vital for our survival. Each system is comprised of many parts – organs and tissues – working together to carry out an important function, such as breathing or digestion. The more we know about how the body works, the better each of us can care for our own personal, amazing, natural machine.

More than four new human bodies enter the world every second – and two die.

UNDER THE SKIN

The body's biggest single organ – the skin – is visible for all to see. Like many other organs, it has several tasks. Skin covers, protects, helps control temperature, and senses touch. The next biggest organ is the liver, in the right side of the torso. It has hundreds of jobs, adjusting levels of blood sugar, minerals and nutrients. Co-ordinating all these parts, and more, is the brain. It receives and sends millions of tiny electrical nerve signals every second through the network of billions of nerve cells.

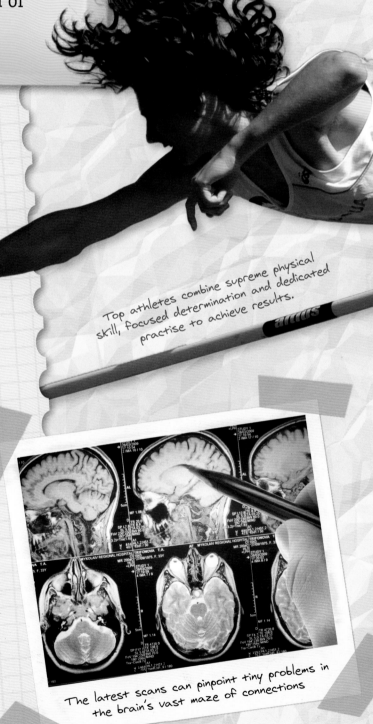

Top athletes combine supreme physical skill, focused determination and dedicated practise to achieve results.

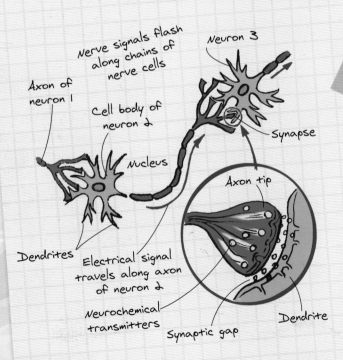

Nerve signals flash along chains of nerve cells

Neuron 3

Axon of neuron 1

Cell body of neuron 2

Synapse

Nucleus

Axon tip

Dendrites

Electrical signal travels along axon of neuron 2

Neurochemical transmitters

Synaptic gap

Dendrite

The latest scans can pinpoint tiny problems in the brain's vast maze of connections

The topics featured in this book are Internet linked.
Visit www.factsforprojects.com to find out more.

MECHANICAL MARVEL

The human body is a mechanical masterpiece capable of incredible feats of strength and movement. At a basic level, our muscles pull bones to move them at joints. It sounds simple, but for each muscle contraction that takes place, dozens of other muscles work to steady the other parts around it, adjust the body's posture, and keep it well balanced. This involves thousands of nerve signals every second passing from the brain's movement centres out to the muscles. There is feedback too, from sensors in the muscles, tendons and skin, and from the eyes, so the brain knows how the movement is progressing.

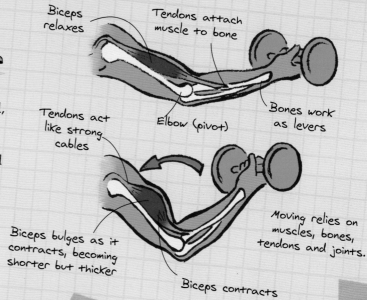

Biceps relaxes

Tendons attach muscle to bone

Bones work as levers

Elbow (pivot)

Tendons act like strong cables

Moving relies on muscles, bones, tendons and joints.

Biceps bulges as it contracts, becoming shorter but thicker

Biceps contracts

Using microscopes, surgeons can perform operations on nerves thinner than this 'l'.

With determination and practise, limb loss can be turned into sporting victory

MEDICAL WONDERS

Treating, healing and curing the sick or diseased body are among the greatest achievements of modern science. Every year sees new kinds of scans and diagnostic tests, better medical drugs to ease pain and suffering, and advances in surgery that seem almost miraculous. There is also the rise of genetic treatments. These aim to change the genes – the instructions for how the body develops and runs itself. In the future, gene therapies may get to the very core of how the body works, why it goes wrong, and how it can be mended.

SKIN, HAIR AND NAILS

Without its ever-renewing skin, the body's delicate inner parts and fluids would be exposed to all kinds of knocks, scrapes, dirt and germs. The skin is one of the body's busiest parts. Its outer layer, the epidermis, completely replaces itself every month to cope with constant wear and tear. It is also the biggest sense organ, responding to physical contact as well as heat, cold, vibration, pressure and pain.

Did you know?

Almost every second, even when the body is asleep, dozens of tiny, worn skin flakes fall from its surface. Towelling yourself dry after a shower removes many millions of them. If you collected all these flakes, in one year they would fill three average 10-litre buckets.

An average adult's skin has an area of about 2 sq m, which is approximately the size of a single bed.

✳ SKIN deep

Skin colour comes from microscopic cells know as melanocytes dotted through the base of the epidermis. They make tiny particles of the very dark-brown pigment melanin, which they pass to other epidermal cells around them. Most people have the same number of melanocytes, about 1000 in every square millimetre of skin. The colour of skin depends on how active these cells are, which is determined by genes. Exposure to ultra-violet rays makes melanocytes more active, darkening the skin to protect against sunburn.

Sweat duct This thin tube connects the sweat gland in the dermis to the pore at the surface. Watery sweat cools the body as it dries.

Sweat pore

Almost half a litre of water is lost every day by evaporation through the epidermis and sweating.

Sebaceous gland makes sebum

Skin comes in all shades from almost white to dark brown

Hair root Hairs grow at their root, from a deep infolded pocket of the epidermis known as a hair follicle. Each follicle has a sebaceous, or skin-oil, gland.

Subcutaneous fat layer

Find out more about what skin is made of and how it can be damaged by visiting www.factsforprojects.com and clicking on the web link.

Fingernails grow about 3 mm each week, and faster in summer than winter. Toenails grow slightly more slowly.

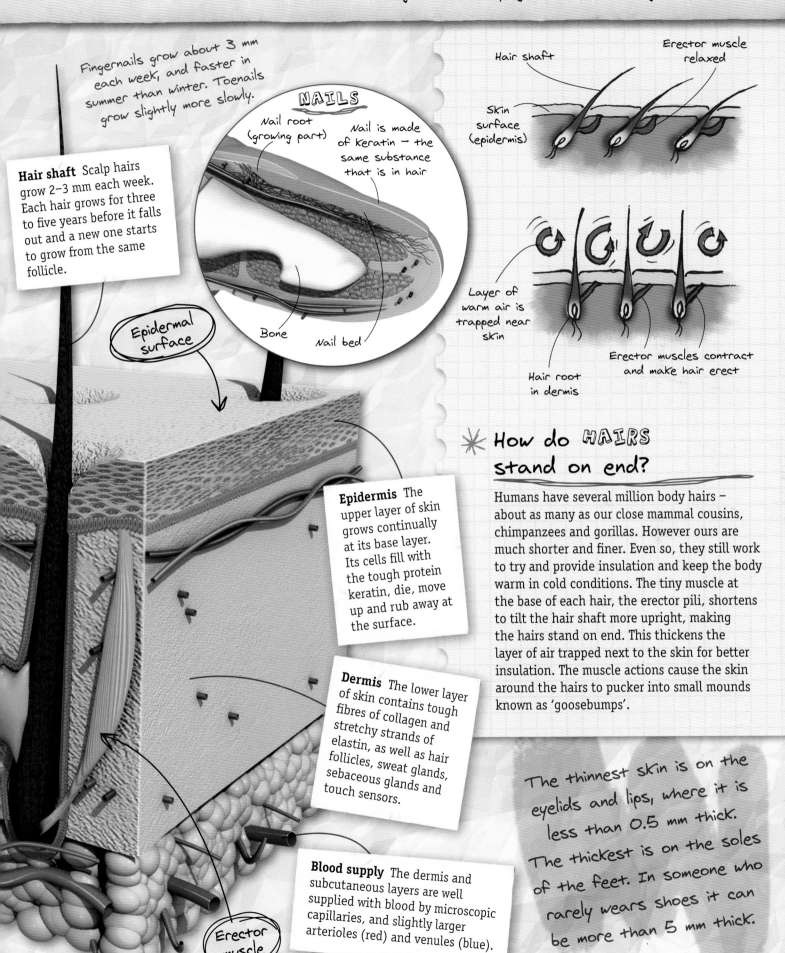

NAILS

Nail root (growing part)

Nail is made of keratin — the same substance that is in hair

Bone

Nail bed

Hair shaft Scalp hairs grow 2–3 mm each week. Each hair grows for three to five years before it falls out and a new one starts to grow from the same follicle.

Epidermal surface

Hair shaft

Erector muscle relaxed

Skin surface (epidermis)

Layer of warm air is trapped near skin

Hair root in dermis

Erector muscles contract and make hair erect

Epidermis The upper layer of skin grows continually at its base layer. Its cells fill with the tough protein keratin, die, move up and rub away at the surface.

Dermis The lower layer of skin contains tough fibres of collagen and stretchy strands of elastin, as well as hair follicles, sweat glands, sebaceous glands and touch sensors.

Blood supply The dermis and subcutaneous layers are well supplied with blood by microscopic capillaries, and slightly larger arterioles (red) and venules (blue).

Erector muscle

✳ How do HAIRS stand on end?

Humans have several million body hairs – about as many as our close mammal cousins, chimpanzees and gorillas. However ours are much shorter and finer. Even so, they still work to try and provide insulation and keep the body warm in cold conditions. The tiny muscle at the base of each hair, the erector pili, shortens to tilt the hair shaft more upright, making the hairs stand on end. This thickens the layer of air trapped next to the skin for better insulation. The muscle actions cause the skin around the hairs to pucker into small mounds known as 'goosebumps'.

The thinnest skin is on the eyelids and lips, where it is less than 0.5 mm thick. The thickest is on the soles of the feet. In someone who rarely wears shoes it can be more than 5 mm thick.

SKELETON AND BONES

The 206 bones of the skeleton are pale, shiny and very active. They continually renew their structure, replenish their mineral reserves, and repair tiny chips or cracks. Over time, bones can even respond to the body's movement patterns by adding strengthening fibres along the most recent lines of greatest stress.

Did you know?

Few parts of the body are as active as the jelly-like marrow inside most bones. This has a rich blood and nerve supply. Red marrow makes all the new cells for the blood – red blood cells are produced here at the rate of up to three million per second.

There are 22 main bones in the skull. But only one can move – the lower jaw. The others are fixed firmly together along wavy joints known as sutures.

INSIDE A BONE

Most bones have a very hard, dense outer layer that provides most of the strength. Inside this is a more lightweight, honeycomb-like spongy layer. The marrow cavity is at the centre.

Bones grow and adapt to the stresses put on the body. For example, in a tennis player, they become stronger and more robust in the arm that holds the racquet.

Periosteum (outer covering)

Marrow and blood vessels

Spongy or cancellous bone

Hard or compact bone

Head The end of a long bone is known as the head. It is ball-shaped to fit and move inside its joint. It is covered by smooth cartilage, as shown on pages 14–15.

When upright the body can support lots of extra weight

✳ MECHANICAL marvel

Unlike nearly all of our mammal relatives, the human skeleton's greatest strength is in the vertical direction. As the body's main upright support, the vertebral (spinal) column of backbones is designed to cope with being squashed or compressed in a downwards direction, since all the body parts 'hang' from it. If we stay fairly upright, we can carry quite heavy loads. But bending or leaning in the wrong way, or for too long, puts huge extra stresses on the spine and causes backache and injury.

Most bones are in the extremities (the hands and feet). Each wrist has 8, then 5 in the palm and 14 in the thumb and fingers. The ankle has 7, with again 5 in the foot and 14 in the toes.

Learn the names of the bones in your body and test yourself on an interactive skeleton by visiting www.factsforprojects.com and clicking on the web link.

SKELETON

Mandible (lower jaw)

Chest The 12 pairs of ribs protect the heart and lungs. The top seven pairs ('true ribs') join to the sternum. The next three pairs ('false ribs') attach to the lowest of the true ribs. The bottom two pairs ('floating ribs') attach only to the spine.

The bulkiest bone is the pelvis (hip bone). The femur (thigh bone) is the longest, and makes up one-quarter of the body's height. The smallest is the stirrup, deep in the ear.

Spine There are 33 vertebrae, or backbones, in the spinal column. Most of them can move slightly against their neighbours to give overall flexibility.

Bones may seem hard and dry, but they are on average one-fifth water.

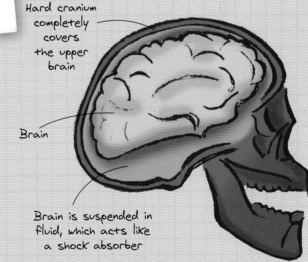

Hard cranium completely covers the upper brain

Brain

Brain is suspended in fluid, which acts like a shock absorber

Carpal (wrist) bones

Leg bones The femur (thigh bone) connects to the tibia and fibula bones of the lower leg at a complex knee joint. The tibia, or shinbone, is sturdier than the slender fibula.

Patella (kneecap)

✳ How do BONES protect you?

Bones offer protection as well as support. The delicate brain is completely surrounded by the bones of the skull. Above the brain is the dome of the cranium, formed from eight large, curved, bony plates. Its curved shape provides great strength to resist knocks and pressure. Below the brain are the 14 bones of the face and cranial floor. For added protection, we have skin and hair on the outside, and on the inside is a liquid called cerebrospinal fluid. This surrounds the brain so it 'floats' and is cushioned against impact. In the hip region, the curved, flared, bowl-shaped pelvis cradles and protects the parts inside the lower body, including the bladder and the female reproductive organs.

Ankle The hard, bony lumps on the outside and inside of the ankle region are not true ankle (tarsal) bones. They are the outward-projecting bases of the fibula and tibia in the lower leg.

The bones of the ankle are called tarsal bones.

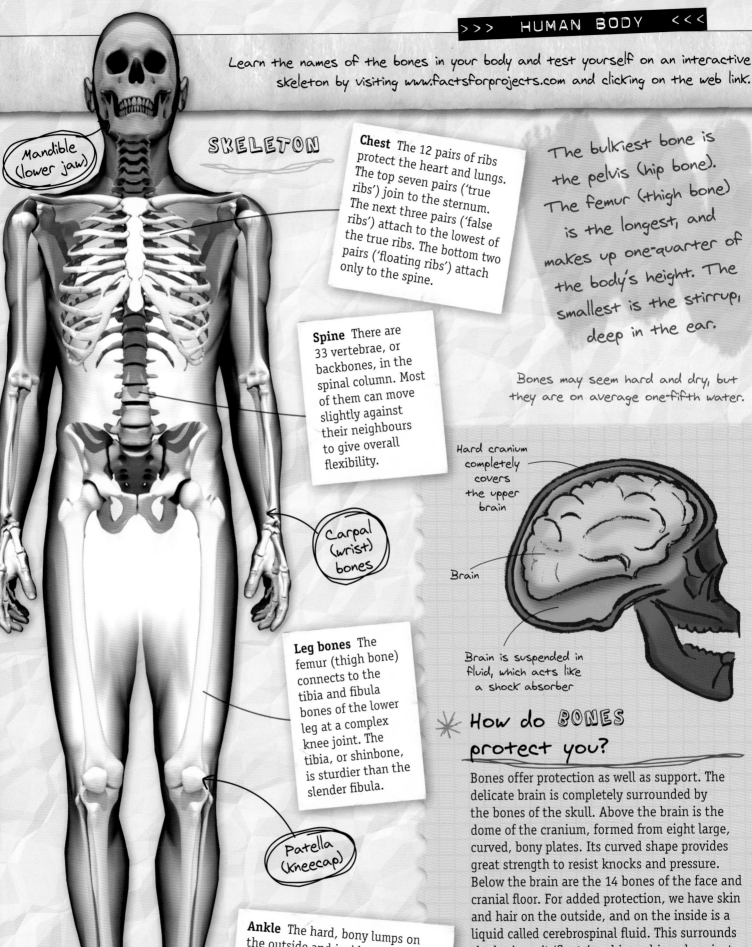

MUSCLES AND MOVEMENT

In relatively fit people who are not overweight, muscles make up about two-fifths of body weight. Despite this bulk, and compared to many other multi-tasking parts of the body, muscles have just one main function – to shorten, or contract. With more than 640 muscles to control, the brain learns to make most movements and actions almost automatically.

Did you know?

People who are very fit and strong do not have more muscles. Everyone has the same number. However their individual muscles can develop bigger muscle fibres for greater strength and an improved blood flow bringing more oxygen and energy.

The most powerful muscles for their size are the temporalis and masseter, the main jaw muscles.

Fascicle Myofibres are about as thin as hairs. A bundle of myofibres is called a fascicle.

INSIDE A MUSCLE

Group of fascicles (bundles)

Body of muscle The main body, or belly, contains many bundles of muscle fibres. Each of these fascicles is wrapped in a sheath, the perimysium. Around the whole muscle is a covering called the epimysium.

Myofibrils Each myofibre (muscle fibre) is composed of many even thinner myofibrils (muscle filaments), where contraction is based.

✳ MUSCLE pumping

Several main types of myofibril (muscle filaments) make up muscle fibres. FT (fast twitch) fibres contract quickly and powerfully, but they soon run out of energy and become fatigued rapidly. ST (slow twitch) fibres take longer to shorten, and do so less powerfully, but they can keep going for longer. Every muscle in each person has its own mix of ST and FT fibres. The proportions are possessed from birth and partly determine whether that person will be good at 'explosive' actions such as weightlifting or long-jump, or longer-term, high-stamina activities such as distance running.

Tiny muscles, such as those inside the inner ear, have just a few dozen muscle fibres. Big muscles in the leg have many thousands.

Muscles are controlled by nerve signals coming from the brain along motor nerves.

The more we use our muscles, the stronger they become

Discover more about the muscular system by visiting www.factsforprojects.com and clicking on the web link.

MUSCLES OF THE BODY

Jaw muscles

Pectoralis

Abdominal muscles
There are three main layers of abdominal muscles, often called 'abs'. These give strength to the front of the abdomen, where there are no bones.

Tendons pass through wrist

Muscles of the femur
Four large, powerful muscles at the front of the thigh, known as the quadriceps femoris, bend the hip to pull the thigh up and forwards, and also straighten the knee.

As well as skeletal (striped) muscles that move bones, there are also visceral (smooth) muscles in the guts, bladder and other inner organs, and cardiac muscle in the heart.

Tendon connects muscle to bone

Gastrocnemius

Ankle tendons Tendons from muscles in the lower leg pass through the ankle to pull the foot and toe bones. The wrist has a similar arrangement between the forearm muscles and fingers.

Tibialis anterior muscle

How do MUSCLES work?

The long bones of the arms and legs are the body's mechanical levers. Their joints, such as the shoulder, elbow, hip and knee, are the mechanical versions of pivots. When a muscle such as the biceps muscle in the upper arm contracts, it pulls the lower arm bone near the elbow joint. The biceps may only shorten by a few centimetres, but since its point of attachment is so near the elbow, it moves the lower arm bones to swing the hand through an arc of many centimetres. In engineering, this extra movement is known as mechanical advantage.

Biceps relaxes

Tendons attach muscle to bone

Tendons act like strong cables

Elbow (pivot)

Bones work as levers

Biceps contracts

Biceps bulges as it contracts, becoming shorter but thicker

The bulkiest muscle in the body is the gluteus maximus in the buttock and upper rear thigh. It pulls the thigh backwards when walking, running and jumping.

The body's smallest muscle is the tiny stapedius, attached to the stirrup bone in the ear (see page 32–33).

JOINTS

Individual bones are just one part of the skeletal system. For bones to move, they must be linked at joints. There are more than 300 joints in the body, varying from the largest single joint, the knee, to the smallest, the knuckles. In a joint, bone is covered by smooth cartilage and lubricated by fluid. Each joint is purpose-designed in shape and size to allow enough movement in certain directions, but without too much freedom, which would diminish strength and stability.

Did you know?

Tiny amounts of thick, slimy synovial fluid are found in joints. Each knee – the biggest joint – has less than a teaspoon of this. If the synovial fluid was collected from all the body's joints, it would hardly half-fill a coffee mug.

Compound joints such as the jaw can move from front to back, and side to side, but cannot rotate.

✳ BENT double

Joints that are well used stay flexible and smooth-moving for many years. This is partly due to the muscles that work them keeping their strength and so preventing a joint from over-flexing, which causes tears and swelling. However, too much use, and especially unnatural actions such as twisting that are necessary in certain sports, can build up many small areas of damage. These can develop into joint problems such as osteoarthritis.

TYPES OF JOINTS

Ball-and-socket joints allow bones to rotate in all directions, creating a range of movements. Hinge joints only allow movement forwards and backwards.

Saddle joint The base of the thumb has a saddle joint, like two horse saddles against each other. This allows tilting and sliding.

The smallest joints are between the smallest bones – the hammer, anvil and stirrup inside the ear.

Jaw (compound)

Shoulder (ball-and-socket)

Fingers (hinges)

Elbow (hinge)

Hip (ball-and-socket)

The most flexible joints are also the least stable. Both the shoulder and hip are ball-and-socket designs. But the shoulder is much more flexible, making it more likely to dislocate or 'pop out'.

Knee (hinge)

Ankle (compound)

Ballet dancers work to become incredibly flexible yet strong

To test your knowledge of the joints in your skeleton and their locations visit www.factsforprojects.com and click on the web link.

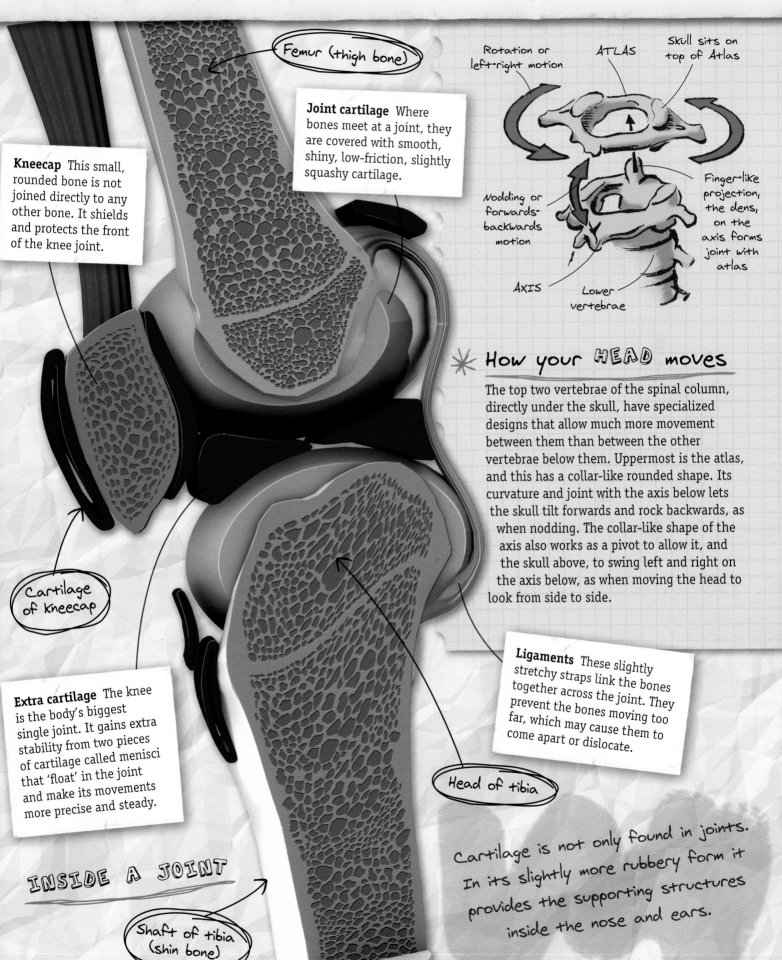

Femur (thigh bone)

Joint cartilage Where bones meet at a joint, they are covered with smooth, shiny, low-friction, slightly squashy cartilage.

Kneecap This small, rounded bone is not joined directly to any other bone. It shields and protects the front of the knee joint.

Cartilage of kneecap

Extra cartilage The knee is the body's biggest single joint. It gains extra stability from two pieces of cartilage called menisci that 'float' in the joint and make its movements more precise and steady.

INSIDE A JOINT

Shaft of tibia (shin bone)

Rotation or left-right motion

ATLAS

Skull sits on top of Atlas

Nodding or forwards-backwards motion

Finger-like projection, the dens, on the axis forms joint with atlas

AXIS

Lower vertebrae

How your HEAD moves

The top two vertebrae of the spinal column, directly under the skull, have specialized designs that allow much more movement between them than between the other vertebrae below them. Uppermost is the atlas, and this has a collar-like rounded shape. Its curvature and joint with the axis below lets the skull tilt forwards and rock backwards, as when nodding. The collar-like shape of the axis also works as a pivot to allow it, and the skull above, to swing left and right on the axis below, as when moving the head to look from side to side.

Ligaments These slightly stretchy straps link the bones together across the joint. They prevent the bones moving too far, which may cause them to come apart or dislocate.

Head of tibia

Cartilage is not only found in joints. In its slightly more rubbery form it provides the supporting structures inside the nose and ears.

LUNGS AND BREATHING

The body can last for days without food, and even a day or two without water. But without oxygen from the air, its cells and tissues start to die within minutes. The lungs are the vital organs that take oxygen from air and pass it to the bloodstream. They do the equally important task of getting rid of the waste product carbon dioxide. If this builds up in the body, it could kill even faster than a lack of oxygen.

Did you know?

If all of the airways in the body were joined end to end, from the main windpipe to the tiniest bronchioles, they would stretch more than 50 kilometres. From the windpipe to the air sacs (alveoli) is about 15 branchings.

The branching airways, from the windpipe to the main bronchi, then smaller bronchi and bronchioles, are known as the 'respiratory tree'.

In both lungs, there are more than 300 million tiny air chambers called alveoli. They provide a tennis-court-sized area for taking in oxygen and getting rid of waste carbon dioxide.

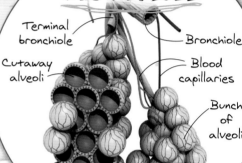

BRONCHIOLES AND ALVEOLI

Terminal bronchiole

Bronchiole

Cutaway alveoli

Blood capillaries

Bunch of alveoli

✳ PHEW!

Stored air in bottles or tanks allows humans to travel to, and work in, all kinds of hazardous environments where otherwise we would soon suffocate – die from lack of oxygen. These places include under the water, deep mines and caverns, wells, swamps and volcanoes. Here gases such as methane and carbon dioxide would otherwise poison the body. Breathing apparatus is especially important for firefighters since the air around them is smoke-laden, lacking in oxygen, and also so hot it would burn the airways.

Deep in the lungs The smallest airways – bronchioles – are thinner than hairs. They lead to bunches of microscopic bubble-like air chambers called alveoli, where oxygen passes into the blood.

At rest, most people breathe 12–15 times each minute.

Blood system Pulmonary (lung) arteries (blue) bring stale blood from the heart. After this is refreshed with oxygen it goes back to the heart along pulmonary veins (red).

Diaphragm This muscle sheet works under instructions from the brain's automatic breathing or respiratory centre.

The stale air from a scuba diver's lungs bubbles into the water

To see an animated diagram of how breathing works visit www.factsforprojects.com and click on the web link.

Air from a sneeze travels at more than 200 km/h.

BREATHE IN

Chest expands

Ribs swing up and out

Diaphragm contracts, becoming flatter

BREATHE OUT

Chest contracts

Ribs fall down and back

Diaphragm relaxes and curves

How do LUNGS breathe?

Only breathing in is muscle-powered. It happens when the sheet of muscle below the lungs, called the diaphragm, contracts from its relaxed dome shape and becomes flatter. The bases of the lungs are pulled down, making the lungs bigger. At the same time, rib muscles contract to make them tilt up and outwards, again stretching the lungs. These movements suck fresh air into the lungs. To breathe out, the diaphragm and rib muscles relax and the lungs recoil to their smaller size.

Nasal chamber Inside the nose, incoming air is filtered by nose hairs, and warmed and humidified. Germs stick to the mucus lining the chamber.

Trachea Also called the windpipe, this bendy tube carries air between the throat above and the lungs below. The voicebox is at the top.

When we speak quietly, we breathe out up to ten times more slowly than when we breathe out without speaking. The air passes between two ridges — the vocal cords — inside the voicebox (larynx). This flow makes the cords vibrate to produce sounds.

Heart

Lung lobes The right lung has three main sections (lobes) branching from the left bronchus. The left lung has only two, because it is smaller. This is due to a scooped-out shape that accommodates the heart.

An average breath at rest moves around half a litre of air in and out of the lungs. After great activity, deeper breaths and a faster breathing rate can increase the throughflow of air by 30 times.

Lower lobe of left lung

Lower ribs

HEART AND BLOOD

The heart is not much more than a simple blood pump. However, it is an amazingly reliable and efficient one, beating perhaps three billion times during a lifetime. The heart is also very responsive in its speed and output. During great activity it can pump more than seven times the amount of blood than it does when the body is at rest.

Did you know?

The distribution of blood around the body is very 'one-sided'. At any moment about three-quarters is in the veins, on the way back to the heart. One-fifth is in the arteries and only one-twentieth is in the capillary network.

An average adult human body contains between 4 and 5 litres of blood.

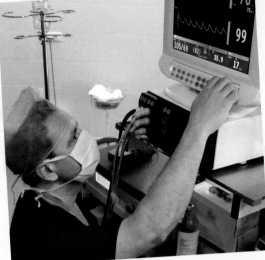

The electrocardiogram (ECG) machine records heartbeats

✳ Tick TOCK Tick TOCK

The heart has many litres of blood passing through it every minute. But it cannot use this blood for its own supplies of oxygen, energy and nutrients for the ever-demanding muscles in its walls. Blood within the heart undergoes waves of very high pressure and fast movement, which would burst delicate capillaries. Also blood in the right side of the heart is low in oxygen. So there are specialized vessels called coronary arteries, which convey fresh, high-oxygen blood from near the start of the aorta (main artery) and branch to distribute it to the heart muscles.

Superior vena cava

Pulmonary arteries

Right atrium Each upper small chamber, the atrium, has thin, floppy walls. It receives blood from the veins and squeezes to push it through the atrio-ventricular valve to the ventricle below.

Heart wall The walls of the heart are made of cardiac muscle. Unlike skeletal muscles, this can work non-stop without tiring.

LOCATION

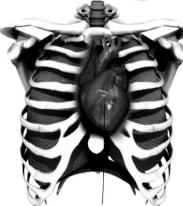

Two-thirds of the heart is on the left side of the body

Right ventricle The thick-walled, muscular lower chamber pumps low-oxygen blood out to the lungs.

Inferior vena cava

Watch a heart beating and find out why heart attacks happen by visiting www.factsforprojects.com and clicking on the web link.

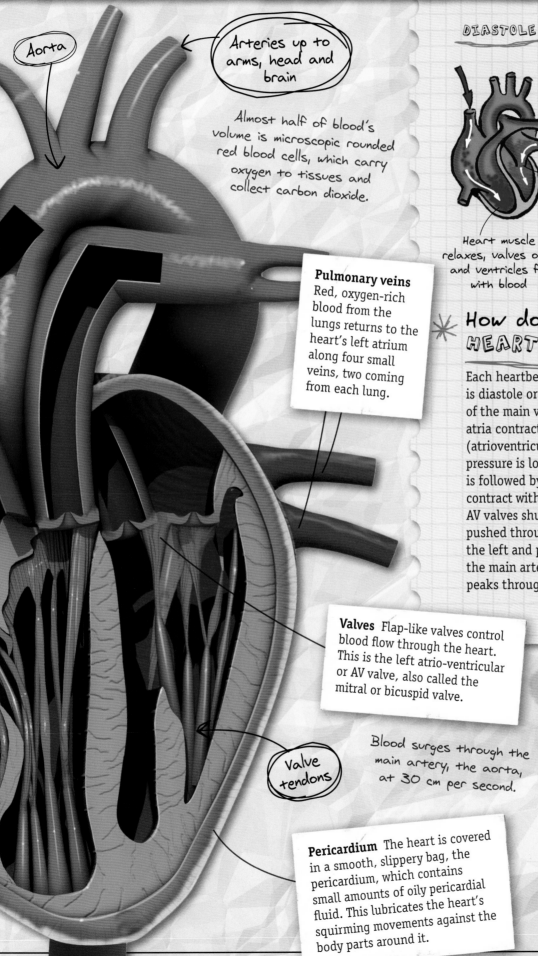

Aorta

Arteries up to arms, head and brain

Almost half of blood's volume is microscopic rounded red blood cells, which carry oxygen to tissues and collect carbon dioxide.

Pulmonary veins
Red, oxygen-rich blood from the lungs returns to the heart's left atrium along four small veins, two coming from each lung.

Valves Flap-like valves control blood flow through the heart. This is the left atrio-ventricular or AV valve, also called the mitral or bicuspid valve.

Valve tendons

Blood surges through the main artery, the aorta, at 30 cm per second.

Pericardium The heart is covered in a smooth, slippery bag, the pericardium, which contains small amounts of oily pericardial fluid. This lubricates the heart's squirming movements against the body parts around it.

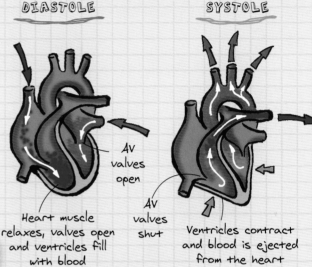

DIASTOLE

SYSTOLE

AV valves open

Heart muscle relaxes, valves open and ventricles fill with blood

AV valves shut

Ventricles contract and blood is ejected from the heart

How does the HEART pump?

Each heartbeat has two main phases. One is diastole or relaxation. The wall muscles of the main ventricle chambers relax as the atria contract to push blood through the AV (atrioventricular) valves into them. Blood pressure is lowest at this time. Diastole is followed by systole. The ventricle walls contract with great force, which makes the AV valves shut to prevent backflow. Blood is pushed through more valves, the aortic on the left and pulmonary on the right, out into the main arteries. This is when blood pressure peaks throughout the whole system.

At rest, the average heart beats about 70 times each minute and pumps out around 5 litres of blood. After strenuous exercise this can rise to 30-plus litres per minute.

TEETH

As well as being covered with the body's hardest substance, enamel, teeth have the shortest growing time of almost any body part. Adult or permanent (second-set) teeth take several months to enlarge from tiny buds to their full size, from the ages of about six to 18 years, depending on their position in the mouth. Then they hardly enlarge at all – for what could be 100 years.

Did you know?

The adult set of teeth is supposed to number 32. The rearmost four molars or cheek teeth – left and right, in upper and lower jaws – are called wisdom teeth. But in about one person in three, the wisdom teeth never erupt, or develop enough to show above the gum.

Ancient Romans carved false teeth for people in ivory – from the teeth of elephants.

✳ OPEN WIDE!

Over thousands of years, average human jaws have become smaller, while the teeth have done so at a lesser rate. This means many people have crowded teeth, or the teeth grow crooked as they try to force their way into too small gaps between their neighbours. Various kinds of dental appliances or 'braces' help to make sure the teeth grow straight and even. This not only improves their appearance, but also makes them easier to clean and evens out the pressures on them during eating.

Incisor teeth The eight incisors are in two sets of four in the upper and lower jaws. They have straight, sharp edges, like small chisels, and are suited to nibbling and gnawing.

Canine teeth There are four canines, two upper and two lower, each behind the incisors. These tall, pointed teeth are adapted to tear and rip up chunks of food.

As the body ages, the gums start to shrink or recede to expose more root and make the crown appear longer, hence the saying 'long in the tooth'.

Crown and root Each tooth has a crown visible above the gum and a root that anchors it into the jawbone. The crown and root meet at the gum line which is known as the neck of the tooth. The crown is covered by enamel.

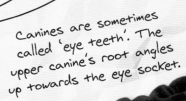

Canines are sometimes called 'eye teeth'. The upper canine's root angles up towards the eye socket.

Arch-shaped lower jaw or mandible

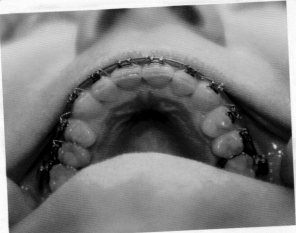

Dental braces help teeth to grow straight and evenly-spaced

For some fun facts about teeth visit www.factsforprojects.com and click on the web link.

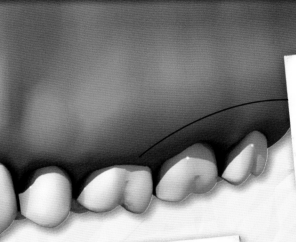

Gums The gum or gingival tissue is soft but hard-wearing, and very active. It replaces itself rapidly as eating wears it away.

The pulp contains nerves that warn of too much pressure, which might crack the tooth.

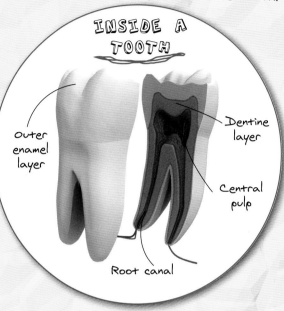

INSIDE A TOOTH

Outer enamel layer

Dentine layer

Central pulp

Root canal

Premolars In each side (left and right) of each jaw (upper and lower) are two premolar teeth. They help the molars with crushing and chewing and also have a shear-like action.

Incisors and canines usually have one root. But premolars and molars often have two, perhaps three, or even more. Each person's tooth anatomy is as individual as fingerprints.

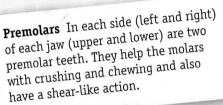

Molars At the rear of the jaw on either side are three molar teeth. They are broad with cusps (points) for powerful chewing.

Double-rooted first molar

✳ How do TEETH grow?

Well before birth, the beginnings of two sets of teeth are formed inside the jaw bone. The first of the 20 baby, milk or deciduous teeth appear or 'erupt' on average after 6–9 months, and all of them have grown by three years. The adult or permanent teeth then start to replace them from around six to seven years of age, pushing out the first teeth as they grow. By the age of 20 years, all of the adult teeth have appeared – except perhaps for the wisdom teeth (see opposite).

Unless it is very yellow, pitted and decaying, the colour of enamel does not indicate its hardness.

Jawbone The tooth root is fixed almost rigidly into the jaw with a living form of cement plus strong periodontal fibres.

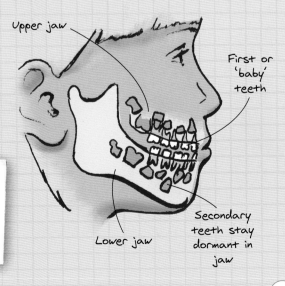

Upper jaw

First or 'baby' teeth

Lower jaw

Secondary teeth stay dormant in jaw

DIGESTIVE SYSTEM

A typical person eats more than half a tonne of food each year – about ten times the body's entire weight. Food is not just nutrients and raw materials for growth and repair of wear and tear. It also brings high-energy substances, especially sugars and starches, and to some extent fats, that provide the power for life processes, keeping warm and moving about.

Did you know?

The human digestive tract, from mouth to anus, is usually said to be about 9 metres in length. However, this is when its wall muscles are relaxed and floppy, which is usually after death. When the muscles are tensed and working, the tract is nearer 5–6 metres.

Chewing food makes it soft and easy to swallow, starts its physical breakdown, and also mixes it with saliva, which begins its chemical breakdown.

✳ Healthy GUTS

Some of the most important foods we eat give very little nutrition and energy, yet they are vital for healthy digestion. They contain plenty of fibre or 'roughage'. Our digestive system cannot break this down, but fibre gives the food bulk so that it can be gripped and moved easily through the system. It also absorbs various unwanted substances which could otherwise cause damage, and protects against problems such as certain forms of cancer. Fresh fruits and vegetables are the best sources of fibre, and we should aim to eat at least 'five a day'.

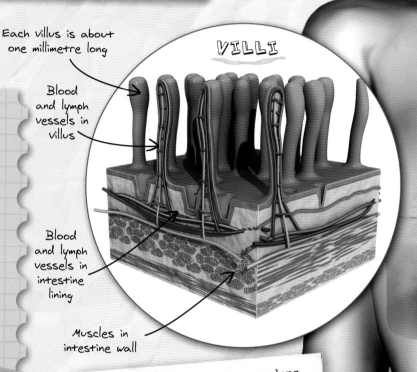

VILLI

Each villus is about one millimetre long

Blood and lymph vessels in villus

Blood and lymph vessels in intestine lining

Muscles in intestine wall

Small intestine and villi The very long, but narrow and winding, small intestine has millions of tiny finger-shaped villi inside. These greatly increase the surface area for absorbing digested food.

Ascending colon

Colon The large intestine or colon forms a 'frame' around the small intestine. It absorbs water and minerals, and compresses the wastes for removal.

Fruit and vegetables are essential to keep our bodies healthy

Find more amazing facts, pictures and videos about the digestive system by visiting www.factsforprojects.com and clicking on the web link.

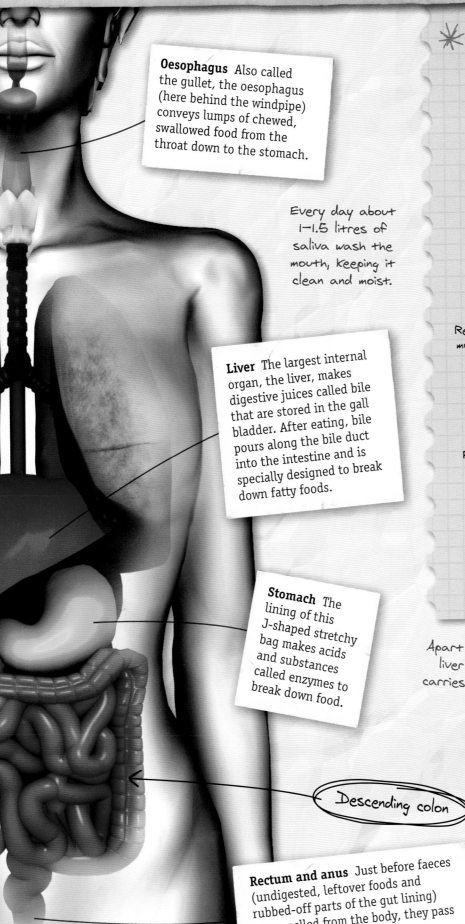

Oesophagus Also called the gullet, the oesophagus (here behind the windpipe) conveys lumps of chewed, swallowed food from the throat down to the stomach.

Every day about 1–1.5 litres of saliva wash the mouth, keeping it clean and moist.

Liver The largest internal organ, the liver, makes digestive juices called bile that are stored in the gall bladder. After eating, bile pours along the bile duct into the intestine and is specially designed to break down fatty foods.

Stomach The lining of this J-shaped stretchy bag makes acids and substances called enzymes to break down food.

Descending colon

Rectum and anus Just before faeces (undigested, leftover foods and rubbed-off parts of the gut lining) are expelled from the body, they pass into the rectum.

✳ How does PERISTALSIS work?

Peristalsis is the wave-like contraction of muscles all along the walls of the gut or digestive tract. It begins when food enters the oesophagus, and ends when leftover wastes come out of the anus. Circular muscle fibres behind the gut contract to make the passageway narrower, forcing the contents along. This circular contraction gradually moves along the tract, pushing the contents ahead of it. At the same time lengthways or longitudinal muscle fibres shorten in front of the contents, to pull the gut backwards past the contents.

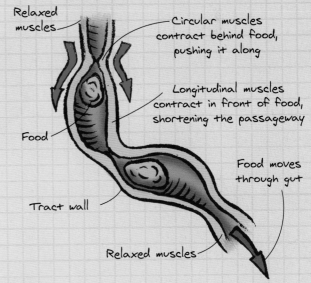

Relaxed muscles

Circular muscles contract behind food, pushing it along

Longitudinal muscles contract in front of food, shortening the passageway

Food

Food moves through gut

Tract wall

Relaxed muscles

Apart from busy muscles (including the heart), the liver generates most the body's warmth, as it carries out hundreds of chemical actions on foods.

On average, food spends less than one minute being chewed in the mouth and a similar time in the oesophagus, but 2 to 4 hours in the stomach, 4 to 6 hours in the small intestine, and 12 hours or more in the large intestine.

WASTE REMOVAL

Every second, blood collects a huge variety of wastes from the body's chemical processes (metabolism). One is carbon dioxide, expelled from the lungs. Almost all the other wastes are filtered from the blood by the kidneys. Each kidney contains about one million tiny filter units known as nephrons, which are marvels of micro-engineered water disposal and recycling.

Did you know?

To filter wastes efficiently, the kidneys receive a huge supply of blood – far more for their size than other organs. Up to one-quarter of all the blood pumped out from the heart passes through them, so that all the body's blood flows through the kidneys in four or five minutes.

To replace water lost in breath, sweat, faeces and urine, the body should take in at least 2.5 litres daily.

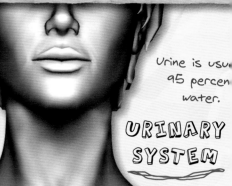

Urine is usu... 95 percen... water.

URINARY SYSTEM

✳ New KIDNEYS for old

In kidney failure, the filtering mechanisms become less efficient and wastes build up in the blood to dangerous levels. One solution is dialysis, where blood is led away from the body along a tube and through a machine that carries out most of the filtering functions. This usually takes 2–3 hours, 2–3 times each week. In peritoneal dialysis, fluid is put into the abdomen (stomach) through a tube, usually for several hours a day, to soak up or absorb the wastes, and is then drained away. A long term solution is a kidney transplant, which can last 20 years or more.

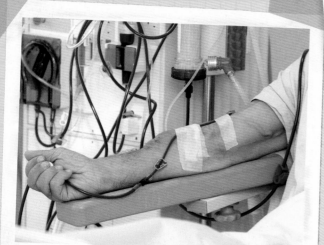

Dialysis replicates many functions of the kidneys

Blood supply The renal artery, which takes blood to the kidney, and the renal vein, which takes away cleaned blood, are short but very wide.

Kidneys The left kidney is slightly higher than the right one. Both are in the upper rear of the abdomen, near the backbone.

Ureter Urine from the kidney passes along the narrow, muscular ureter tube to the bladder. The urine is propelled by peristaltic waves, similar to those that move food in the digestive system.

Bladder This muscle-walled bag can expand gradually to hold more urine. To release the contents, a muscular ring called the urinary sphincter relaxes at the start of its exit tube, the urethra.

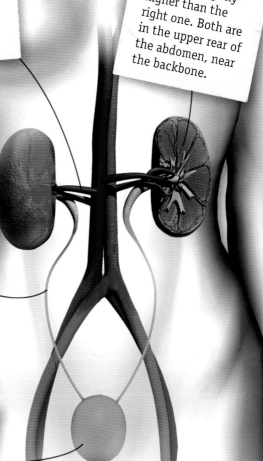

Read more about how kidneys filter blood and keep your body balanced by visiting www.factsforprojects.com and clicking on the web link.

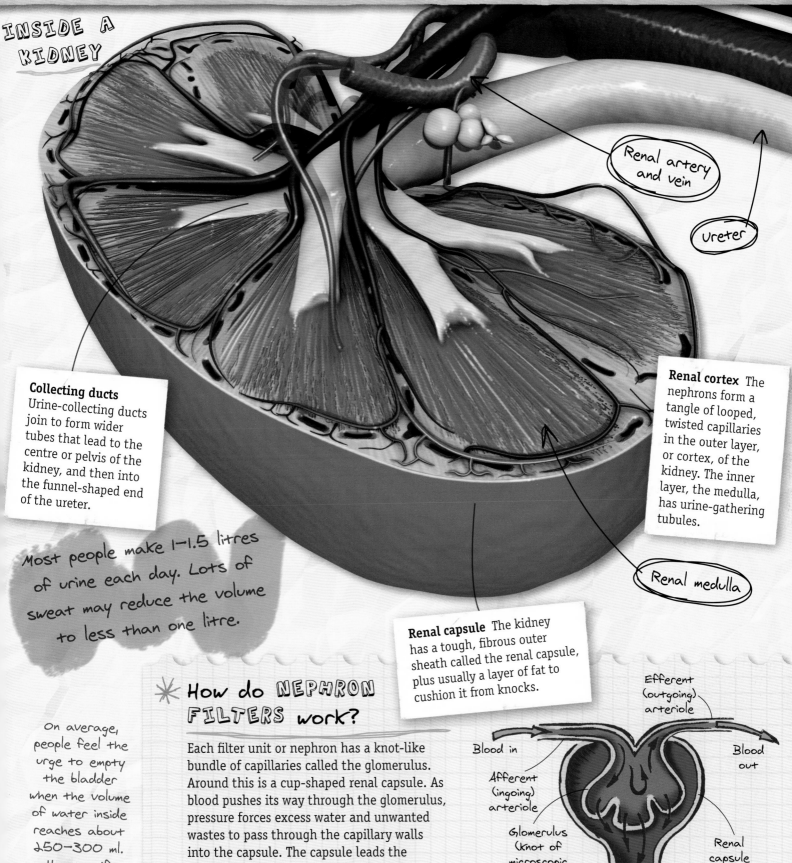

INSIDE A KIDNEY

Renal artery and vein

Ureter

Collecting ducts
Urine-collecting ducts join to form wider tubes that lead to the centre or pelvis of the kidney, and then into the funnel-shaped end of the ureter.

Renal cortex The nephrons form a tangle of looped, twisted capillaries in the outer layer, or cortex, of the kidney. The inner layer, the medulla, has urine-gathering tubules.

Renal medulla

Most people make 1–1.5 litres of urine each day. Lots of sweat may reduce the volume to less than one litre.

Renal capsule The kidney has a tough, fibrous outer sheath called the renal capsule, plus usually a layer of fat to cushion it from knocks.

✳ How do NEPHRON FILTERS work?

On average, people feel the urge to empty the bladder when the volume of water inside reaches about 250–300 ml. However if desperate, the bladder can hold almost twice this amount.

Each filter unit or nephron has a knot-like bundle of capillaries called the glomerulus. Around this is a cup-shaped renal capsule. As blood pushes its way through the glomerulus, pressure forces excess water and unwanted wastes to pass through the capillary walls into the capsule. The capsule leads the resulting liquid, first-stage filtrate, into a pipe called the proximal tubule. At a later stage much of the water from the filtrate is taken back into another capillary system, to concentrate the wastes as urine.

Efferent (outgoing) arteriole

Blood in

Blood out

Afferent (ingoing) arteriole

Glomerulus (knot of microscopic capillaries)

Renal capsule

Proximal tubule

First-stage filtrate

LYMPH SYSTEM

Lymph is a pale fluid that is the body's 'alternative' blood. It has up to twice the volume of blood, but no dedicated pump and no outgoing vessels. It starts as the general fluid that oozes from and around cells, tissues and tubes, propelled slowly by the body's movements and the massaging effect of pulsing blood vessels. Lymph collects in tubes or ducts, passes through nodes or 'glands', and eventually rejoins the blood in the upper chest.

Did you know?

Lymph has no special way of taking up oxygen, as blood does in the lungs. But otherwise its tasks are quite similar to blood, including delivery of nutrients and collecting wastes. In particular, lymph has an important role in fighting disease. If an infection strikes, its white blood cell numbers can go up by more than 1000 times.

There are about 500 lymph nodes or 'glands' in a typical human body.

Cervical lymph nodes in neck

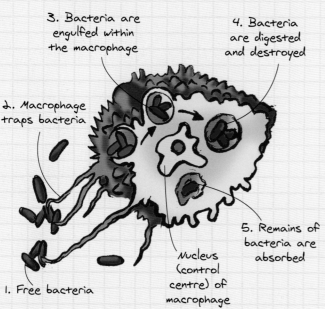

3. Bacteria are engulfed within the macrophage

4. Bacteria are digested and destroyed

2. Macrophage traps bacteria

5. Remains of bacteria are absorbed

Nucleus (control centre) of macrophage

1. Free bacteria

✳ How do WHITE BLOOD CELLS work?

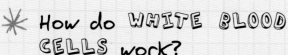

There are several kinds of white blood cell, each with different tasks in defending the body. Macrophages or 'big eaters' consume germs such as bacteria, which are much smaller than them. The macrophage is flexible and puts out long arm-like 'feelers' to search for germs. Any that are found are pulled towards the main cell body, which flows around them to engulf them. Slowly, digestive substances dissolve away the germs. One macrophage can eat more than 100 bacteria during its lifetime of a few months.

Main lymph ducts Smaller lymph vessels gather to form large lymph ducts in the chest and empty the lymph into large veins near the heart.

Axillary lymph nodes These are the nodes in the armpits. Like the cervical nodes in the neck, their tenderness and swelling is often an early sign of a developing infection.

Lymphoid tissues Collections of germ-fighting lymphoid tissues are found in several areas, including the nose and throat (see tonsils, opposite), and lumps called Peyer's patches along the intestine.

To discover more about the lymphatic system and see some brilliant pictures visit www.factsforprojects.com and click on the web link.

The 'adenoids' (pharyngeal tonsils) are lymph-rich tissues at the lower rear of the nasal chamber. The 'tonsils' (palatine tonsils) are similar lumpy tissues in the upper throat.

Adenoids

Tonsils

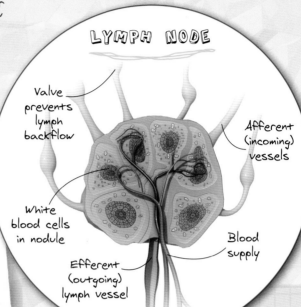

LYMPH NODE

Valve prevents lymph backflow

Afferent (incoming) vessels

White blood cells in nodule

Efferent (outgoing) lymph vessel

Blood supply

If the body is exercising hard, it may call upon the extra blood stored in the spleen. As muscle contractions squeeze this blood into circulation, there may be a sharp pain in the spleen area called a 'stitch'.

Inside a lymph node
Each node has several ducts coming in and just one leaving. It contains smaller nodules inside its strong outer capsule. White cells gather in the cortex and other spaces within the nodules.

Some of the 'memory' white cells in the lymph and immune (self defence) system that recognize germs are almost as old as the body itself.

Spleen In the upper left abdomen behind the stomach, the spleen is the largest lymph organ. It recycles old red blood cells and also stores blood.

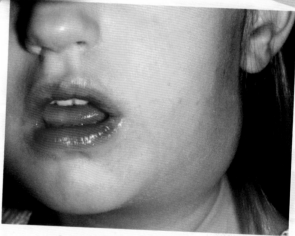

Sometimes when we get an infection our 'glands' swell up

There are usually about 5000–15,000 white blood cells in one pinhead-sized droplet of blood. There are many more red cells — generally around 5 million in the same droplet.

Smallest lymph vessels in fingers

✳ Down in the MOUTH

When the body battles an infection, much of the action takes place in the lymph nodes – commonly called 'glands'. These become centres of germ warfare as white blood cells amass to attack, engulf, disable and destroy invading microbes (see opposite). The dead germs and white cells accumulate and burst open, releasing their fluids. All of these processes make the lymph nodes swell to perhaps five times their healthy size, becoming hot and tender, and sometimes very painful.

HORMONES AND GLANDS

The brain and nerves are one of the body's two control and coordination systems. The other is the hormonal or endocrine system. This uses substances called hormones made in endocrine glands. Most hormones take effect over long periods, from hours to years. They control energy use, levels of minerals and other blood substances, as well as growth and development.

Did you know?

Many hormones work in a 'push-pull' way, with one opposing another to produce finely balanced control. The hormone calcitonin, from the thyroid gland, reduces blood levels of calcium, while parathyroid hormone from the parathyroid glands increases its level.

Pituitary gland Just beneath the lower front of the brain, the pituitary makes about ten hormones. Some of these control the actions of other hormone glands. Pituitary growth hormone affects the whole body.

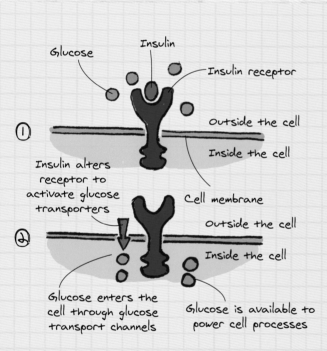

Glucose

Insulin

Insulin receptor

Outside the cell

Inside the cell

①

Insulin alters receptor to activate glucose transporters

Cell membrane

Outside the cell

②

Inside the cell

Glucose enters the cell through glucose transport channels

Glucose is available to power cell processes

In 1922, medical workers Frederick Banting and Charles Best showed how injections of insulin could treat the condition of diabetes. Their work has saved millions of lives.

Liver makes three hormones

Kidneys The hormone renin from the kidney has widespread affects on the amounts of fluids in the body, especially how much water they contain. In this way it controls the amounts of urine produced and also affects blood pressure.

Adrenaline from the adrenal glands is one of the fastest-acting hormones, causing effects in just a few seconds.

How do HORMONES work?

Most hormones seem to work using receptors that are sited in the outer 'skins' or membranes of microscopic cells. The hormone particle or molecule slots into its specially shaped receptor like a key fitting in a lock. This alters the shape of the receptor and triggers further actions. For example, the hormone insulin fits into its receptors in the membranes of certain cells. This activates channel-like gateways further along the cell membrane, allowing in high-energy glucose molecules, to be stored or to drive various life processes within the cell.

Sex hormones In females (shown here), the ovaries produce hormones such as oestrogen and progesterone, which control egg release and the reproductive cycle. The male testes make testosterone, which stimulates sperm development.

To find out more about the hormones in your body and what they do visit www.factsforprojects.com and click on the web link.

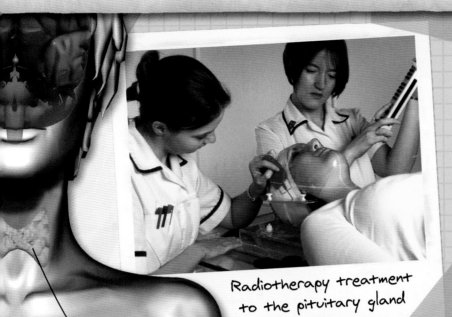

Radiotherapy treatment to the pituitary gland

✳ HORMONE trouble

Rarely, hormonal glands become under- or overactive, perhaps because they develop a growth or tumour. An overactive thyroid gland produces too much thyroxine, which makes chemical processes through the whole body speed up. This is known as hyperthyroidism and the person becomes nervous and anxious, and loses weight. If the thyroid gland is underactive, in hypothyroidism, the body becomes slow and lethargic, lacking energy. These types of problems can usually be treated with medical drugs, surgery, or radiotherapy (X-rays or similar) to shrink the growth.

Thyroid and parathyroid glands In the front of the neck, the thyroid releases thyroxine. This controls the speed at which cells around the body take in energy and carry out their internal processes.

The hormone melatonin from the brain's pineal gland controls our sleep-wake cycle.

Adrenal gland on top of kidney

Adrenal gland The adrenal is really two glands in one. Hormones from its cortex affect water and mineral balance, and how the body copes with stress. The hormone adrenaline from its medulla activates the 'fight-or-flight' response.

Pancreas Insulin and glucagon, both produced in this gland, control the level of blood glucose by a 'push-pull' system.

Uterus (womb) Hormones control pregnancy and birth. During labour, the hormone oxytocin makes the uterus contract, then instructs the body to release milk. It even helps the mother to bond with her baby.

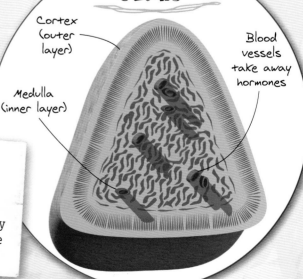

ADRENAL GLAND

Cortex (outer layer)

Medulla (inner layer)

Blood vessels take away hormones

EYES AND SIGHT

For most people, sight is the dominant sense. It brings almost as much information into the brain as all the other senses combined. The eyes can be regarded as outgrowths of the brain. With 120 million-plus light-detecting cells each, they can see clear detail, a wide range of colours, and perceive depth or distance, giving 3D vision.

Did you know?

The six eyeball-moving muscles are among the hardest-working and fastest-reacting in the body. As we watch a speeding object go past, the eyes do not follow it smoothly. They scan it in less than one-tenth of a second, flick sideways to where it will be in another split second, scan it there, and so on – all under automatic brain control.

A jelly-like fluid called vitreous humour fills the eyeball and gives it shape. It is one of the clearest, most transparent substances known.

Optic nerve from eye to brain

Almost all babies are born with bluish eyes. The eventual colour takes a few months to develop.

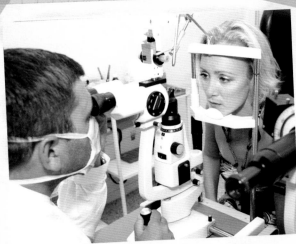

An optician using equipment to give an eye test

✳ It's all CLEAR now

In some people the lens is slightly too weak or strong for the eyeball, or the eyeball itself is slightly over- or under-sized. This results in blurred vision. The solution is an extra lens in front of the body's own one to help with focusing. The extra lens may be a small contact lens on the cornea, or a bigger lens in glasses. In some cases the cornea itself can be sculpted to the correct shape by 'melting' away parts of it with a very precisely aimed laser beam – the cornea soon recovers.

Eye-moving muscles
Also called the extrinsic eye muscles, these are strap-shaped and curve around the eyeball. They anchor at the rear inside of the eye socket, or orbit.

Even when we sleep, the eyeballs flick around as though watching a scene. This is REM, rapid eye movement or 'dreaming' sleep.

Choroid (blood supply layer)

The retina's rod cells see only black and white, but work well in dim conditions. The cones detect colours and fine detail, but need bright conditions to function.

Test your vision with lots of fun activities by visiting www.factsforprojects.com and clicking on the web link.

Superior eye-moving muscle

Fovea (yellow spot) This is the area where an image focuses for us to see it most clearly, with lots of cone cells.

Ciliary muscles and lens The lens hangs in a circle of ciliary muscles. When these contract they allow the lens to bulge and focus on nearby objects. Relaxed, they make the lens thinner for seeing distant objects.

How does the IRIS control light levels?

In the middle of the iris is what looks like a black spot. In fact it is a hole, the pupil, which lets light rays into the eye. When light levels are low, the iris muscles alter the iris shape to make the pupil larger, or dilated. This means more light rays can enter the eye for a clearer view. In bright conditions the muscles change the iris shape to shrink or constrict the pupil to prevent too much light from damaging the delicate retina. These reflex changes also alter the distance range, or depth of field, which we can see clearly.

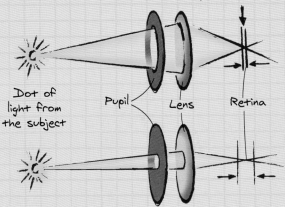

DILATED PUPIL

Plenty of light enters the eye, but it can focus on only a narrow range of distances

Dot of light from the subject

Pupil   Lens   Retina

CONSTRICTED PUPIL

Less light enters but the eye sees a bigger range of distances clearly

Iris The coloured part of the eye, the iris, is a collar-like ring of two sets of muscles. These contract in opposition to alter its size.

Cornea (clear domed front of eye)

The detailed pattern of streaks, pigments and blood vessels on the iris is unique in every eye. Iris scans can be more useful than fingerprints since they are very difficult to fake.

Sclera The sclera is the tough, pale outermost coating, or sheath, of the eyeball. At the front it is seen as the 'white' of the eye.

Retina This inner layer contains more than 100 million rod cells and six million cone cells, which turn patterns of light rays into nerve signals.

EARS AND HEARING

Like sight, hearing is an 'at a-distance' sense. It tells us what is happening away from the body, and gives us warning of approaching dangers such as speeding traffic. The ear flap on the side of the head may look important, but it is only a funnel-shaped guide for invisible sound waves to the inner parts of the ear. The vital process of turning sound vibrations into nerve signals happens in these inner parts.

Did you know?

Sound travels through air at about 340 metres per second. So a sound coming from the side reaches one ear a fraction of a second before the other (and is louder in the first ear too). The time difference is less than 1/1500th of a second – but the brain can detect it.

Temple skin

Skull bone

If the ear detects very loud sounds, in a split second the tiny stapedius muscle attached to the stirrup bone contracts to damp down its vibrations, and prevent damage to the cochlea.

Outer ear (pinna) This collects more sound waves from in front than behind. By comparing volume or loudness, the brain can work out where the sounds come from.

Entrance to ear canal

Ear structure The outer ear flap has an inner framework of bendy cartilage (gristle). It can flex if knocked or rubbed, rather than breaking, as bone might.

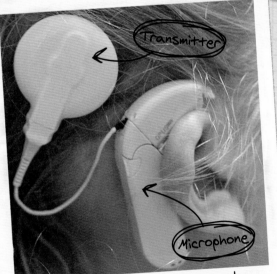

Transmitter

Microphone

A person fitted with a cochlear implant wears a microphone and a transmitter

✳ Loud and CLEAR

Treatments for hearing problems depend on the cause. In conductive problems the sound vibrations have trouble reaching the cochlea in the inner ear. One solution is a hearing aid on or in the ear flap, to boost incoming sounds, make their vibrations larger, and aim them at the eardrum. Some hearing problems are based in the cochlea itself. One answer is an electronic microchip called a cochlear implant that detects vibrations, turns them into tiny electrical signals, and feeds them directly into the nerve to the brain.

To read more about how ears work and how they help us balance visit www.factsforprojects.com and click on the web link.

Semi circular canals These three C-shaped tubes, each at right angles to the others, are filled with fluid that swirls around as the head moves. Sensors detect the motion to help with balance.

The hair cells in the cochlea are arranged in two long rows, inner and outer, to help us distinguish the volume and pitch of sounds. There are between 15,000 and 20,000 hair cells in each cochlea.

Vestibular nerve from balance organs

Cochlea This snail-shaped organ changes the vibrations of sounds into patterns of nerve signals to send to the brain.

Eustachian tube to throat

Eardrum

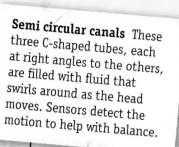

Ear bones A chain of three tiny bones, the ear ossicles, link the eardrum to the cochlea. They are called the hammer, anvil and stirrup. They pass along vibrations caused by sound waves hitting the eardrum, also making them more forceful.

Middle ear space The tiny ossicle bones bridge the air-filled middle ear between the eardrum and cochlea, held in place by minute, delicate ligaments and tendons.

Humans can hear sound pitches between about 20 and 20,000 vibrations per second. Dolphins and bats can hear up to 200,000.

✳ How do we HEAR?

Sound waves are areas of high and low pressure travelling through the air. They hit the eardrum and make it vibrate. The vibrations pass along the ear bones to the cochlea, causing similar waves of high and low pressure to ripple through the fluid inside. The ripples shake a flexible flap called the tectorial membrane. In this are embedded the tips of microscopic hairs from thousands of hair cells arranged in a spiral strip, the organ of Corti. When the tectorial membrane shakes, the hairs do too, and stimulate the hair cells to make nerve signals. Different parts of the membrane shake for low- or high-pitched sounds.

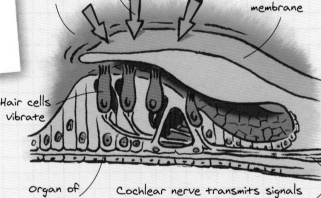

Sound waves in the cochlear fluid cause the tectorial membrane to vibrate

Fluid

Tectorial membrane

Hair cells vibrate

Organ of Corti

Cochlear nerve transmits signals from the hair cells to the brain

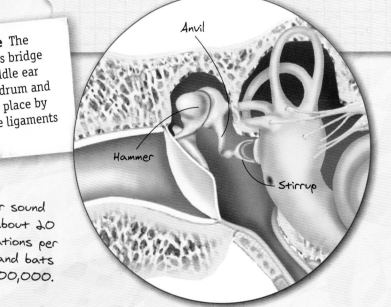

Anvil

Hammer

Stirrup

TASTE AND SMELL

A delicious meal brings the pleasure of lovely odours and excellent flavours. On the other hand, food that has gone 'off' or is rotten makes us wrinkle our noses and grimace in disgust. The nose at the entrance to the breathing system, and the tongue at the start of the digestive system, give early warning about foul air or putrid tastes, so we can take action to avoid them. These two senses work in similar ways, by detecting tiny particles or molecules of smells and flavours.

Did you know?

Smell is far more sensitive than taste. The nose can distinguish more than 10,000 different scents, odours and aromas. The tongue picks up only about five basic flavours. However, it does register differing proportions of these in various foods and drinks.

The five basic taste flavours are sweet, salty, sour, bitter and savoury (umami).

Corpus callosum (connects two sides of brain)

Olfactory bulb
This mass of nerve cells (see opposite) connects to the hair cells below.

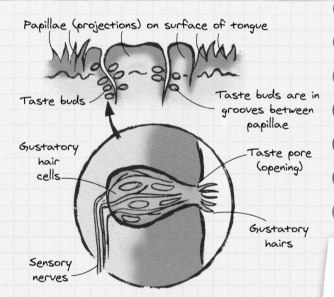

Papillae (projections) on surface of tongue

Taste buds

Taste buds are in grooves between papillae

Gustatory hair cells

Taste pore (opening)

Gustatory hairs

Sensory nerves

Young people have up to 10,000 taste buds. Older people may have only 5000 – one reason why foods taste more bland with age.

Olfactory epithelium hair cells The smell hair cells (see opposite) work when certain flavour substances touch them.

✳ How does TASTE work?

Taste is based in small clusters of microscopic cells called gustatory hair cells. These work in a similar way to olfactory hair cells (see opposite). The information for tastes is carried by different shapes of substances in food and drinks, known as flavourants. As we eat, these flavourants come into contact with micro-hairs sticking out from the hair cells. If certain types of flavourants fit into corresponding receptors on a micro-hair, the hair cell is triggered to make a nerve signal. In the nose, olfactory hair cells detect floating particles in the air called odourants.

Tongue surface Taste buds are mainly along the sides of the tongue and at its tip and upper rear. There are very few in the middle of the upper surface.

Tongue muscle fibres

To test your sense of taste against your sense of smell visit www.factsforprojects.com and click on the web link.

Ventricles The brain is partly hollow. Inside are fluid-filled chambers called ventricles. The cerebrospinal fluid in them helps to distribute nutrients and collect waste.

There are more than 40 million olfactory hair cells in the nose. Some dogs have ten times as many.

Inside the olfactory bulb Nerve signals from the olfactory hair cells are compared, analyzed and 'pre-sorted' before passing along the olfactory tract to the brain.

SMELL SENSORS

olfactory bulb cells

olfactory tract

Skull bone

olfactory epithelium

olfactory hair cells

* Lip SMACKING!

The enjoyment of 'tasty' foods is based largely on smell. As we eat, the taste buds detect flavours on the tongue. But chewing the food also releases many aromas that waft from the back of the mouth, around the gap at the rear of the palate (roof of the mouth) and up into the nasal chamber. Here they are sensed in great detail by the olfactory epithelium. Taste and smell are separate senses, but as we eat, the brain receives masses of information from both. It comes to associate the odours with the flavours, creating an overall 'taste sensation'.

occipital lobe of brain

Up to one in four people are 'supertasters' with greatly increased taste abilities.

Cerebellum This lower rear part of the brain helps with muscle actions and coordination.

Taste combines with sensations such as temperature

BRAIN AND NERVES

Everything associated with the mind and consciousness – thoughts, memories, feelings, emotions, urges, even daydreams – is based in the brain. Despite its appearance, this greyish-pink, unmoving organ is one of the body's busiest. Its 'language' is tiny electrical nerve signals. Every second, millions of them arrive from the senses, flash around the brain, and go out to the muscles.

Did you know?

The average brain weighs 1400 grams, which is 1/50th of body weight. But the brain is so active that it consumes up to one-fifth of all the energy used by the body. The energy is brought by the blood, usually as glucose (blood sugar). A lack of this for just a few seconds can cause problems.

The brain's electrical nerve signals are recorded as an EEG, electro-encephalogram.

Touch centre for skin

Brain map This artificial coloured view of the brain shows how different parts of its outer surface, the cerebral cortex, are important in different tasks. Brown shows the area assisting vision.

occipital lobe

Our brains allow us to draw from memory, expressing emotions

✳ ARTISTIC flair

Where do ideas and creative skills come from? In most people, the brain shares out certain tasks between its two halves. The left side or cerebral hemisphere is mainly concerned with rational thought, logic, and mental activities such as calculations, breaking things down into parts and step-by-step reasoning. The right side takes the lead in inventive thinking, jumping towards whole ideas, linking random thoughts, and appreciation of art and music. Suitable types of 'brain training' can help people to involve both sides of the brain when tackling an activity, often with a better overall result.

Vision area The lower rear of the brain receives and analyzes nerve messages from the eyes, and gives us perception of what we see.

Cerebellum This lower wrinkled part coordinates motor nerve signals going out to the muscles, to make movements smooth, skilled and precisely controlled.

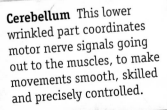

There is no link, in otherwise healthy people, between brain size and intelligence.

Spinal cord (main nerve to body)

Navigate around an interactive brain and learn more about its functions by visiting www.factsforprojects.com and clicking on the web link.

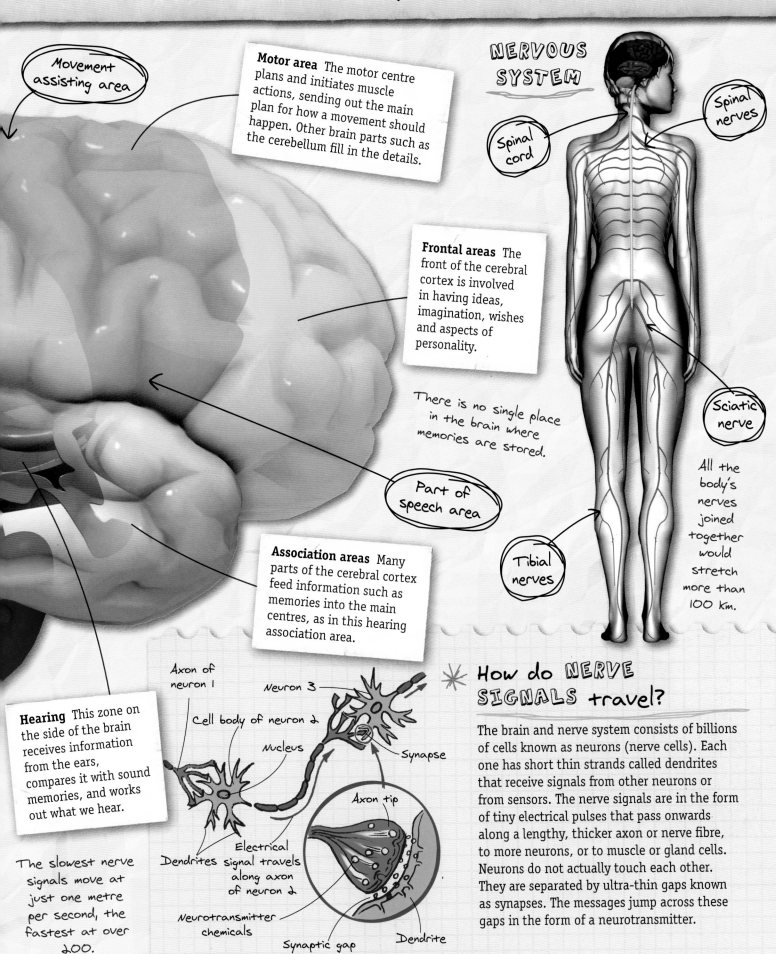

Movement assisting area

Motor area The motor centre plans and initiates muscle actions, sending out the main plan for how a movement should happen. Other brain parts such as the cerebellum fill in the details.

NERVOUS SYSTEM

Spinal cord

Spinal nerves

Frontal areas The front of the cerebral cortex is involved in having ideas, imagination, wishes and aspects of personality.

There is no single place in the brain where memories are stored.

Part of speech area

Sciatic nerve

Association areas Many parts of the cerebral cortex feed information such as memories into the main centres, as in this hearing association area.

Tibial nerves

All the body's nerves joined together would stretch more than 100 km.

Hearing This zone on the side of the brain receives information from the ears, compares it with sound memories, and works out what we hear.

The slowest nerve signals move at just one metre per second, the fastest at over 200.

Axon of neuron 1

Neuron 3

Cell body of neuron 2

Nucleus

Synapse

Axon tip

Electrical signal travels along axon of neuron 2

Dendrites

Neurotransmitter chemicals

Synaptic gap

Dendrite

How do NERVE SIGNALS travel?

The brain and nerve system consists of billions of cells known as neurons (nerve cells). Each one has short thin strands called dendrites that receive signals from other neurons or from sensors. The nerve signals are in the form of tiny electrical pulses that pass onwards along a lengthy, thicker axon or nerve fibre, to more neurons, or to muscle or gland cells. Neurons do not actually touch each other. They are separated by ultra-thin gaps known as synapses. The messages jump across these gaps in the form of a neurotransmitter.

GLOSSARY

Abdomen
The lower part of the main body (torso) that contains organs for digestion, waste removal and, in females, reproduction.

Alveoli
Microscopic air chambers in the lungs where oxygen passes into the blood by flowing through capillaries.

Artery
A blood vessel that carries blood away from the heart.

Axon
The long, thin part of a nerve cell or neuron that carries away nerve signals to pass them on to other nerve cells or to muscles. Also called a nerve fibre.

Bronchi
The main airways in the lungs that lead from the trachea (windpipe) deep into the lung tissues.

Canines
Long, sharp teeth near the front of the mouth, used for jabbing and stabbing.

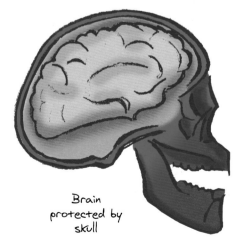

Brain protected by skull

Capillaries
The smallest blood vessels in the body, which allow oxygen and nutrients to pass from the blood into the surrounding cells and tissues. Carbon dioxide and wastes can move the opposite way into the blood.

Cartilage
A strong but slightly flexible body substance, less stiff than bone that forms parts of the skeleton and also covers bones inside joints.

Cerebellum
The lower rear part of the brain, which co-ordinates the nerve signals going out to muscles.

Cochlea
The coiled part deep in the ear that changes the patterns of sound rays that vibrate it into patterns of nerve signals to send to the brain.

Cornea
The domed, clear front of the eye, through which light rays pass and are part-focused, before they go through the lens behind it for fine focusing.

Cortex
The outer layer of an organ such as the kidney or adrenal gland, usually distinct from its inner layer, the medulla.

Dendrites
The short, thin parts of a nerve cell or neuron that gather nerve signals from other cells.

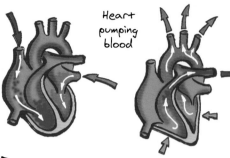

Heart pumping blood

Diaphragm
A sheet of muscle at the base of the lungs between the chest and abdomen. When it contracts, the diaphragm powers the movements of breathing.

Diastole
The phase of the heartbeat when the heart muscles relax and its chambers expand as they refill with blood from the veins.

Glucose
Blood sugar, a type of sugar that contains lots of energy in chemical form. It is obtained from digestion and carried in the blood for use as a general energy source all around the body.

Gluteus maximus
The main muscle in the hip and upper leg which provides the power for movement, such as walking and running.

Gustatory hair cells
Microscopic, smell-sensitive cells inside taste buds that detect flavour particles in foods and drinks, and generate corresponding patterns of nerve signals to send to the brain.

Hormones
Chemical substances made in endocrine glands, which travel in the blood and affect certain parts of the body – the targets – controlling the activity of their cells and tissues.

Incisors
Teeth at the front of the mouth, usually sharp and straight-edged, used for nibbling and gnawing.

Iris
The coloured ring of muscle at the front of the eye that adjusts the size of the hole at its centre, the pupil, according to light levels.

Large intestine
Part of the gut, usually short and wide that absorbs water, vitamins and minerals from digested food, and converts the remains into waste, ready for removal as faeces.

Ligaments
Strong straps that hold together the bones in a joint, so they do not dislocate (come apart or slip out of position).

Lungs
Body parts specialized to take in oxygen from the air and pass it to the blood. Lungs also get rid of waste carbon dioxide from the blood, out into the air.

Mandible
The lower jaw.

Molars
The broad, strong teeth towards the back of the mouth, used for crushing and chewing.

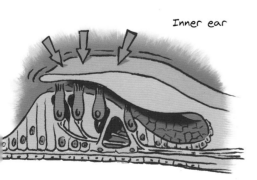

Inner ear

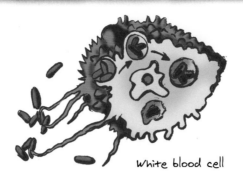

White blood cell

Medulla
The inner layer of an organ such as the kidney or adrenal gland, usually distinct from its outer layer, the cortex.

Nephrons
The microscopic filter units in a kidney, each consisting of a network of capillaries and other tubes that remove wastes and excess water from the blood.

Neurons
Nerve cells that receive, analyze, co-ordinate and pass on nerve signals in the form of tiny pulses of electricity. They usually have short projections called dendrites and a longer one, the axon.

Oesophagus
Also called the gullet, the first part of the gut after the mouth and throat leading down to the stomach.

Olfactory hair cells
Microscopic, smell-sensitive cells inside the nose, which detect odour particles floating in the air and generate corresponding patterns of nerve signals to send to the brain.

Pectoralis
The main muscle in the front chest area, which raises and swings the arm.

Pupil
In the eye, the hole in the ring of muscle called the iris. Light passes through the pupil to the lens inside the eyeball.

Retina
The light-sensitive layer inside the eyeball that changes the patterns of light rays falling on it into corresponding patterns of nerve signals to send to the brain.

Skeleton
The strong supporting framework inside the body, made of 206 bones plus some cartilage.

Small intestine
Part of the gut that is long, thin and coiled, and absorbs nutrients from digested food, into the blood.

Systole
The phase of the heartbeat when the heart muscles contract powerfully to squeeze blood out into the arteries.

Taste buds
Microscopic bundles of cells on the tongue that detect flavour particles in foods and drinks.

Tendons
Strong, tough, rope-like parts that join muscles to bones.

Vein
A blood vessel that carries blood towards the heart.

Vertebrae
Backbones, the long chain of linked bones that make up the spinal column, often called the backbone.

INDEX

Contents

Rocky Worlds

The Earth is an enormous planet. But it is only enormous on our human scale. In the vastness of space it is a tiny place. It is just one member of a whole family of planets. Together with the Sun, these planets make up our Solar System.

Inner planets and outer planets

There are eight planets in our Solar System. Some are smaller than Earth, and some are far larger. Only two planets, Uranus and Neptune, look similar to each other. All the other planets have their own unique features. However, we can divide the planets into two main groups.

The four inner planets drawn at the same scale as the Sun.

The first group is made up of the four planets nearest the Sun: Mercury, Venus, Earth and Mars. These planets have solid, rocky surfaces. They are known as the inner planets, the rocky planets, or the terrestrial planets. These are the planets we look at in this book.

The second group is made up of the four planets much further from the Sun: Jupiter, Saturn, Uranus and Neptune. These gigantic balls of gas are known as the gas giants.

Pluto, a small, icy body beyond Neptune, was classed as a planet until 2006. Then experts at the International Astronomical Union downgraded it to a 'dwarf planet' as it is just one of thousands of similar objects in the same region.

Rocky surfaces

The inner planets are Mercury, Venus, Earth and Mars. They all have surfaces made of solid rock. Mercury is the smallest rocky planet. Its surface is covered with craters, like our Moon. Venus is smothered by a thick atmosphere. Beneath the atmosphere is a surface covered with lava flows. Mars is covered with red-brown rock and dust, and has giant volcanoes and canyons. Earth is very different to these other rocky worlds. It is the only place with oceans of liquid water, moving tectonic plates, and life.

Moons

A moon is a large rocky body that orbits a planet. Earth has one large moon (known as the Moon), and Mars has two tiny moons, Phobos and Deimos.

The inner planets (from back to front, Mercury, Venus, Earth and Mars).

How do we know?
Rocky surfaces

Apart from the Earth, our neighbours in space, Venus and Mars, are the two planets we know most about. Dozens of robot probes have visited each planet, mapping their surfaces, photographing their surface features, and analysing their rocks and atmospheres.

Moving Through Space

All the planets move around the Sun in paths called orbits. They all orbit in the same direction. The orbits are not exactly circular, but slightly squashed. The planets also spin as they move through space.

Planet orbits

The closer a planet is to the Sun, the faster it moves around its orbit. Mercury travels around its orbit twice as fast as Mars, and completes its orbit in one eighth of the time. The Sun is not at the centre of
the squashed orbits of the planets. Instead, it is slightly over to one side. So as a planet orbits the Sun, it moves slightly closer and then slightly further from the Sun. Of all the inner planets, Mercury's orbit is the most squashed.

The orbits of the inner planets (shown as circles).

Spins

The planets also spin as they orbit. Each spins around its axis, which is an imaginary line through the planet. A planet's poles are where its axis comes out through the surface. The Sun lights up the side of a planet nearest to it. As the planets spin, places on their surfaces move in and out of sunlight, giving day and night. The moons also spin as they orbit.

The Earth's spin makes the Sun and stars appear to move across the sky as time passes. You would see the same movement of the Sun and stars from the surfaces of the other planets, but at different speeds.

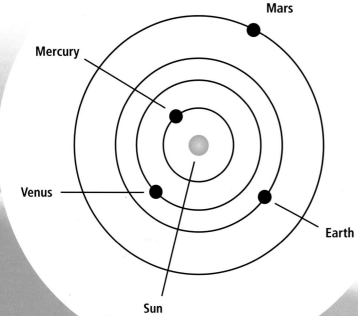

Mars

Mercury

Venus

Earth

Sun

A photograph of the south pole of Venus. It is day on the left side, lit by the Sun, and night on the right side, in shadow.

Days, months and years

The movements of the Earth and Moon give us days, years and months. A day is the time the Earth takes to complete one spin. A year is the time the Earth takes to complete one orbit of the Sun. A lunar month is the time between one New Moon and the next.

Gravity

The force of gravity keeps the Earth and Moon in orbit. Gravity attracts the Earth to the Sun, and the Moon to the Earth. It acts like a string, stopping the Earth and Moon from flying off into space, and making them move in a circle. At the same time, because the Earth and Moon are moving along their orbits, they do not fall towards the Sun or Earth.

SPACE DATA

Inner planet records

Fastest planet: Mercury (48 km per second)

Slowest spin: Venus (243 Earth days)

Fastest spin: Earth (23 hours, 56 minutes)

Longest year: Mars (687 Earth days)

Shortest year: Mercury (88 Earth days)

How the Planets Formed

Astronomers think that all the planets in our Solar System were formed about 4,600 million years ago, soon after the Sun was formed. All the inner planets began life as balls of hot rock.

Birth of the Solar System

Our Solar System formed nearly 5 billion years ago from part of a vast cloud of gas and dust called a nebula. Gravity slowly pulled the gas and dust together into clumps. The clumps also began to spin. Gravity continued to work, pulling the clumps into extremely dense balls of material. Intense heat and pressure in the centre of the balls started nuclear reactions. Energy from the reactions produced heat and light, so the balls began to shine. One of them was our Sun.

Planetesimals

Astronomers think the planets formed from a disc of material left over after the formation of the Sun. This disc was spinning round the Sun, like a spinning CD. It was made of particles of rock, dust and gas. When two particles collided, they sometimes stuck together, forming larger particles. Very slowly, gravity pulled these larger particles together. Eventually large boulders formed. These are known as planetesimals. They were the building blocks of the planets.

The Solar System formed from a cloud of gas and dust like this, million of kilometres across.

Space Facts

- Earth probably had as many craters as Mercury in its early life. They have been wiped away by volcanic eruptions and erosion.

- The planets turned out differently to each other because they contained different mixtures of chemicals, were different sizes, and were different distances from the Sun.

Eventually, gravity pulled the planetesimals together to make the planets. Overall it took 100 million years for the planets to form. The material left over from the disc around the Sun also formed the moons around the planets, and all the other bodies in the Solar System, such as the asteroids and comets.

The early planets

The inner planets had surfaces of molten rock when they were formed. The surface rock gradually cooled as heat from the rock escaped into space. Eventually the liquid rock solidified, forming solid rock. This formed a solid crust all over the planet, with hot rocks underneath.

The space between the planets was filled with planetesimals and smaller lumps of rock. These regularly collided with the young planets, raining down on their surfaces, and smashing holes in them. Gradually, over hundreds of millions of years, the bombardment subsided. We can still see hundreds of these craters on Mercury and the Moon.

Rocks on the surface of Mars, formed when molten rock cooled on the planet's surface.

Mercury

Mercury is the closest planet to the Sun, and the smallest of the inner planets. It is roasted by the Sun's intense heat. We don't know as much about Mercury as we do about most of the other planets. Only one space probe has ever visited the planet, in the 1970s.

Mercury's orbit

Mercury moves around the Sun in a very squashed orbit. At one side of its orbit, Mercury is 70 million kilometres from the Sun, and at the other side, it is just 46 million kilometres from the Sun. Mercury completes an orbit in just 88 Earth days. It travels through space at an incredible 48 kilometres per second. Mercury spins extremely slowly compared to the Earth. It takes more than 58 Earth days to complete one spin.

Strange effects

Mercury's fast orbit and slow spin cause a very strange effect. On Earth, the Sun rises and sets 365 times a year. But on Mercury the Sun rises one year and sets the next year! The time from one sunrise to the next (called a solar day) is 176 days on Mercury. Because a Mercury year lasts just 88 Earth days, on Mercury, you could have two birthdays every day! After a place on Mercury's surface moves into the sunlight, the slow spin means that it stays in the sunlight for an orbit and a half before the sun sets again. Mercury's squashed orbit also means that the Sun sometimes appears to go backwards across the sky.

A map of one side of Mercury made up from photographs taken by the Mariner 10 *probe in the 1970s.*

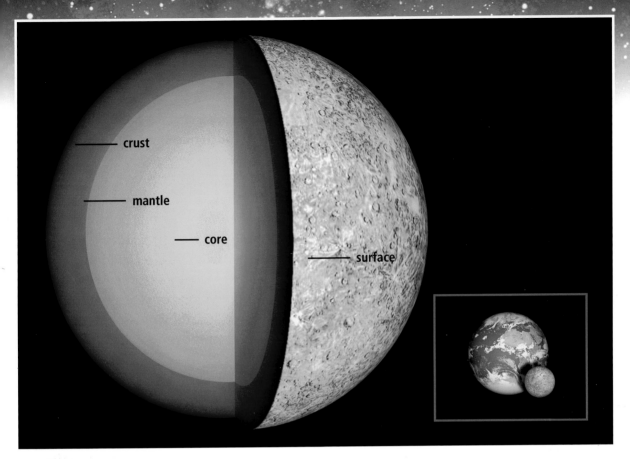

Labels on diagram:
— crust
— mantle
— core
— surface

This is what astronomers think the inside of Mercury looks like.

Mercury's structure

We don't actually know what the inside of Mercury looks like, but we can make some assumptions. We can assume that the internal structure is similar to Earth. That means there is a thin outer crust, a thick mantle underneath, and a core in the centre. Astronomers have calculated the mass of Mercury from observing how it affects the orbit of Venus. From that, they think that Mercury has a dense, iron core that makes up 80 per cent of its mass. Mercury has an extremely thin atmosphere. The *Mariner 10* probe and observatories on Earth have detected oxygen, sodium, hydrogen, helium and potassium in the atmosphere, but so far we don't know how much of each.

SPACE DATA

Mercury

Diameter:	4,879 km
Average distance from Sun:	57,910,000 km
Time to complete one orbit:	88 Earth days
Time to complete one spin:	58.6 Earth days
Gravity at surface:	0.38 x Earth gravity
Surface temperature:	-180°C to 430°C
Number of moons:	0

Mercury: the Surface

Only a little more than half of Mercury's surface has been mapped. The part we have seen looks very much like the Earth's Moon.

Mercury has a complex surface made up of plains and ridges, along with thousands of craters.

Mercury's craters

Most of Mercury's craters were formed in its early life. But some of Mercury's craters are much younger. We know this because we can see lines of rock and dust spreading out from the craters. Craters like this are called ray craters. Mercury's craters were made billions of years ago, but they are still visible because there is no flowing water to wear them away, and no volcanoes to erupt and cover them with lava. Mercury's surface also has flat plains, formed when lakes of molten lava cooled in the planet's early history.

The Caloris Basin

The largest feature on the surface of Mercury is a giant impact crater called the Caloris Basin. It is 1,350 kilometres wide. The gigantic impact that created the basin threw up rings of mountains around the crater, up to 2,000 metres high. The impact was so huge that its effects can be seen on the opposite side of Mercury. Shock waves passed right through the planet like a super-powerful earthquake, creating ripples in the surface on the opposite side.

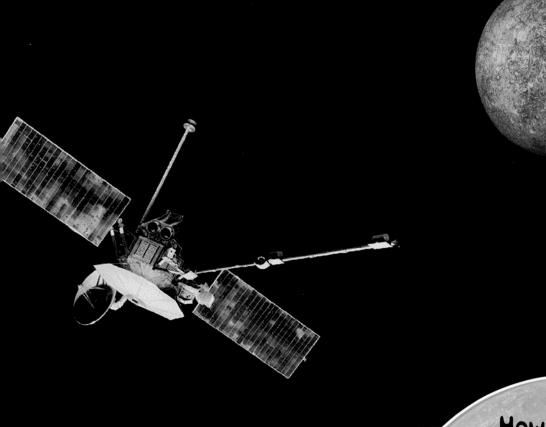

An impression of Mariner 10 *flying past Mercury. The large shade protected the probe from the intense heat of the Sun.*

Mercury cliffs

Mercury's surface also has ridges and lines of cliffs, called scarps. These ridges and scarps are often several kilometres high and hundreds of kilometres long. They were probably formed when Mercury's core cooled and shrank. This made the crust too large for the planet, and it wrinkled up.

Hot and cold

Because Mercury spins so slowly, places on its surface are exposed to the heat of the Sun for a long time. The surface temperature rises to an incredible 430 degrees Celsius. When the same places finally move into the dark, the temperature drops to −180 degrees Celsius. Despite the heat, there may be frozen water in craters near the poles.

How do we know?

Mariner 10

Mercury is the least explored of the inner planets. Only one space probe, *Mariner 10*, has visited, in 1975. *Mariner 10* used the gravity of Venus to get into orbit round the Sun, and it flew by Mercury three times. It took thousands of photographs, but of only one side of the planet. The *Messenger* probe is due to visit Mercury in 2011.

Venus

Venus is the second
planet from the Sun.
It is almost the same
size as the Earth,
and its mass is
almost the same,
too. But Venus is a
very different
world to the Earth.
It has a dry surface,
a thick, choking
atmosphere, and a
surface hotter even
than Mercury's.

Venus's orbit

Venus takes 225 Earth days to
complete one orbit, so its year is
about two-thirds the length of an Earth
year. But the way it spins is very different to the
way the Earth spins. Venus spins extremely slowly. It completes a
spin only once every 243 Earth days. It also spins in the opposite
direction to all the other planets. This is known as a
retrograde spin. It means that the Sun rises
and sets only twice in each year.

*A false-colour image of
the surface of Venus.
The pink areas are the
highlands and the blue
areas are the lowlands.*

Internal structure

Astronomers think that the
internal structure of Venus is
like the internal structure of
the Earth, with a core, mantle
and crust.

SPACE DATA

Venus

Diameter:	12,103 km
Average distance from Sun:	108,200,000 km
Time to complete one orbit:	224.7 Earth days
Time to complete one spin:	243 Earth days
Gravity at surface:	0.9 x Earth gravity
Surface temperature:	464°C
Number of moons:	0

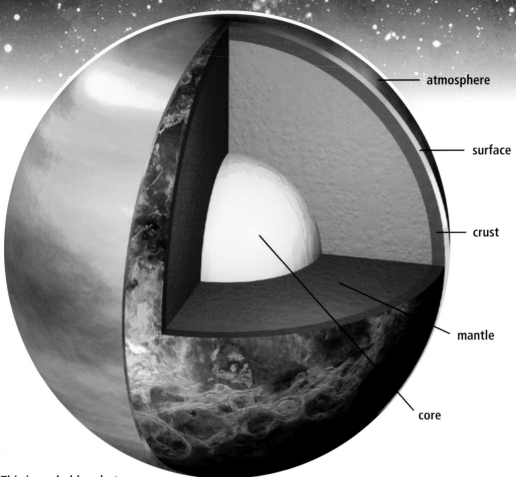

atmosphere

surface

crust

mantle

core

This is probably what the inside of Venus is like. The surface is hidden by the thick atmosphere.

They assume this because it is the almost the size and mass as the Earth, and was formed at the same time. The core is made mostly of iron. Around the core is a mantle of rock. Covering the mantle is a crust. The top part of the mantle is probably molten. This molten rock leaks through the crust in some places, causing volcanoes.

Seeing Venus

Venus is the one of the easiest planets to see. It looks like a very bright star. Because it is closer to the Sun than Earth, it is always close to the Sun in the sky. It can sometimes be seen low in the eastern sky just before the Sun rises, or low in the western sky just after the Sun sets. This is why Venus is known as the morning star or evening star.

The Sun lights only one side of Venus. From Earth we see different amounts of this lit side as Venus moves around its orbit. Sometimes we see nearly a full circle of light, sometimes a semi circle, and sometimes a thin crescent. These shapes are known as phases.

Venus: the Surface

The surface of Venus is quite smooth compared to the surfaces of the other rocky planets. It is dry and strewn with rocks and boulders. It is far too hot for liquid water, which would evaporate instantly. There are very few craters.

Venus volcanoes

Tens of thousands of volcanoes litter the surface of Venus. They may still be active, but because the surface is hidden by cloud, we can't see any eruptions that do happen. Astronomers think that the surface is quite smooth because it has been covered by lava flowing from the volcanoes. This may have happened in the last few hundred million years. The lava has buried most of the craters on the surface. Among the numerous volcanoes are several giant volcanoes which are hundreds of kilometres across.

Volcanic activity has also caused mounds on the surface, where magma under the surface has pushed upwards but not broken through. The mounds, known as pancake domes, are covered with cracks where the surface has stretched. Around the volcanoes are tall, solidified lava falls (like frozen waterfalls).

A three-dimensional image of a volcano on Venus called Maat Mons, mapped by the Magellan *probe using radar.*

Highlands and mountains

Venus has highland regions that stand above the vast flat plains. The two largest regions are called the Ishtar Terra and the Aphrodite Terra. The Ishtar Terra contains Maxwell Montes, the highest mountain on Venus, which is 11 kilometres high (Mount Everest on Earth is just under 9 kilometres high). Aphrodite Terra is as large as Africa. The third highland area, called Beta Regio, contains the two largest volcanoes on Venus, each 4 kilometres high and hundreds of kilometres across. In some places the surface is cracked and rippled, and in others there are deep valleys, probably caused by the surface being pulled apart in the distant past.

Looking down on an impact crater on the Lavinia Planitia plain on Venus.

Venus in the past

In its early life, the surface of Venus may have looked a little like the Earth today. It may even have had oceans of liquid water. But the Sun's heat would have evaporated the water, and also caused the thick atmosphere to form. This is why Venus turned into such a different planet to Earth.

*An impression of the Venus Express **probe** orbiting Venus.*

How do we know?
Magellan and *Venus Express*

Much of our knowledge about the surface of Venus came from the *Magellan* probe that went into orbit around Venus in 1990. It used radar to measure the distance to the surface as it orbited, and so built up a three-dimensional map of the surface. *Venus Express* arrived in 2006 to investigate how the atmosphere works, and to search for volcanic activity.

17

Venus: the Atmosphere

Venus is surrounded by a thick atmosphere, full of clouds that block our view of the surface. The atmosphere is very dense, and it works like a greenhouse, trapping heat from the Sun. An astronaut on the surface of Venus would be crushed by the pressure and roasted by the heat.

Gases of the atmosphere

The atmosphere on Venus is very different to Earth's atmosphere. It contains much more gas than Earth's atmosphere. This makes the atmospheric pressure at the surface ninety times the atmospheric pressure on Earth.

This photograph of Venus's swirling clouds was taken by Mariner 10 *as it flew by on the way to Mercury.*

The gases are different, too. Carbon dioxide makes up ninety-six percent of Venus's atmosphere. Most of the rest is nitrogen. There is no oxygen, so astronauts could not breathe on Venus, even if they could survive the pressure and heat.

Sulphur clouds

Fifty kilometres above the surface of Venus there is a thick layer of cloud, 19 kilometres thick. The clouds never part to let us see the surface. They are made up of droplets of sulphuric acid. Acid rain falls from the clouds, but it never reaches the surface because the drops evaporate as they fall.

At the level of the clouds, severe winds blow at more than 350 kilometres per hour. That's more than hurricane force. Even though it takes 243 Earth days for Venus to complete one spin, the clouds whiz round the planet in just four Earth days.

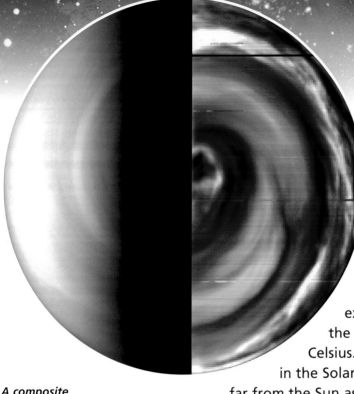

The greenhouse effect

On Earth, carbon dioxide and other gases in the atmosphere trap heat from the Sun. This is known as the greenhouse effect. It keeps the atmosphere warm. The greenhouse effect also happens on Venus. But because the atmosphere is so thick, and mostly carbon dioxide, the effect is extreme. It heats the atmosphere at the surface to a blistering 464 degrees Celsius. This makes Venus the hottest planet in the Solar System, even though it is twice as far from the Sun as Mercury.

A composite photograph of Venus's southern hemisphere. The right half shows heat coming from the clouds.

A photograph of the surface of Venus, taken by the Venera *14 probe in 1982.*

How do we know?

Venera probes

A series of probes launched by the Soviet Union explored Venus in the 1960s, 1970s and 1980s. The first three failed to reach Venus. *Venera 4* was the first probe to enter the atmosphere and send back data. *Venera 7* was the first probe to land successfully and send back data, although it was destroyed by heat and pressure after 23 minutes. *Venera 9* survived long enough to transmit the first-ever photograph of the surface.

ВЕНЕРА-14   ОБРАБОТКА ИППИ АН СССР И ЦДКС

Earth

Earth is the third planet from the Sun. It is the largest of the inner planets. Earth's blue oceans and green vegetation make it look very different to the other planets. It is the only place in the Solar System with oceans of liquid water, with a surface that is constantly changing, and, as far as we know, with life.

The Earth from space. The vast oceans give the Earth its nickname, the 'Blue Planet'.

Earth's orbit and spin

The Earth completes one orbit every year, or 365.26 days. The orbit is almost circular. The Earth completes one spin every 23 hours and 56 minutes.

Earth's structure

The Earth is a giant ball of rock, made up of four layers. We stand on the top layer, which is called the crust. Under the Earth's continents, the crust is 35 kilometres thick on average. It is only a few kilometres thick under the oceans. Under the crust is the mantle. This is nearly 3,000 kilometres thick, and it makes up about three-quarters of the mass of the Earth. The rocks in the top layer of the mantle are partly molten because they are so hot. They flow very slowly, which makes the crust above move about. You can find out more about the moving crust on page 22.

Beneath the mantle is the core, which is divided into the inner core and outer core. Together they are about 7,000 kilometres wide. The core is made mostly of iron. The outer core is molten, and the inner core is solid.

The early Earth

When the Earth formed, its surface was molten. Gradually heat escaped into space from the surface. This made the surface cool and solidify, forming a crust. Meteorites smashed holes in the surface, releasing lava from underneath, and keeping the surface hot. It is likely that one massive collision smashed off a piece of Earth, forming the Moon. At the time the Earth was covered with craters, like Mercury is today. There was no atmosphere, no oceans, no mountain ranges, no rivers, and no life. Over billions of years the Earth has transformed into the planet we know today.

SPACE DATA

The Earth

Diameter:	12,756 km
Average distance from Sun:	149,600,000 km
Time to complete one orbit:	365.3 days
Time to complete one spin:	23 hours 56 minutes
Gravity at surface:	9.81 m/s^2
Surface temperature:	-70°C to 55°C
Number of moons:	1

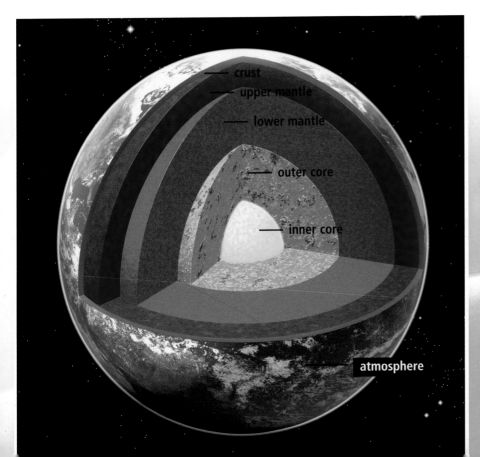

- crust
- upper mantle
- lower mantle
- outer core
- inner core
- **atmosphere**

We know about the internal layers of the Earth by measuring how shock waves from earthquakes bounce around inside it.

Earth: the Surface

The Earth's surface is very different to the surfaces of the other rocky planets. The main differences are due to water. It fills the oceans, forms ice caps, and cuts river valleys. The Earth's surface is always changing, too. New crust is made, mountains are built up, and the landscape is worn away.

Oceans, rivers and ice

Oceans cover two-thirds of the Earth's surface, and contain 97 per cent of all the Earth's water. The Pacific Ocean covers nearly half the surface on its own. On the land, flowing rivers cut valleys and deep canyons into the surface. They also build up features, such as floodplains and deltas. Ice rivers called glaciers also cut valleys in the mountains, and ice forms sheets thousands of metres thick at the poles.

The San Andreas Fault in California, USA, where two tectonic plates slide slowly past each other.

Tectonic plates

The Earth's surface is the top of its outer layer, the crust. The crust is made up of several giant pieces, called tectonic plates. Movements in the molten rock under the crust make the plates move very slowly. This movement is called continental drift. As far as we know, the Earth is the only planet with tectonic plates. Earthquakes happen when the moving plates become jammed and then move suddenly.

Over hundreds of millions of years the plates have moved thousands of kilometres around the globe. Millions of years ago the continents were all bunched together, before they moved to their positions today.

Building mountains

In some places the edges of two plates move towards each other. The edges of the plates crumple up, forming giant mountain ranges such as the Himalayas and the Andes. Mountains are also built up by volcanoes. These normally happen at the edges of tectonic plates, where molten rock is forced to the surface.

Earth Facts

Earth's features

● The Himalayas were pushed up when the Indian tectonic plate collided with the Asian plate. The mountains are still rising by about 6 millimetres per year.

● The Earth's tectonic plates move at a few centimetres a year — about the same speed that your fingernails grow.

Eroding away

The landscape is worn away by a process called erosion. Rocks are broken up by the heat of the Sun, by freezing water, and by being hit by other rocks blown by the wind or carried by water. The loose rock is carried away by the wind, water or pulled downhill by gravity.

The changing surface

Together, the moving tectonic plates and erosion have created all the features on the land, such as mountain ranges, river basins, valleys and plains. In millions of years' time they will have created a completely new surface that we would not recognise.

A satellite view of mountains of the Tibetan Plateau, which was pushed up as India collided with Asia.

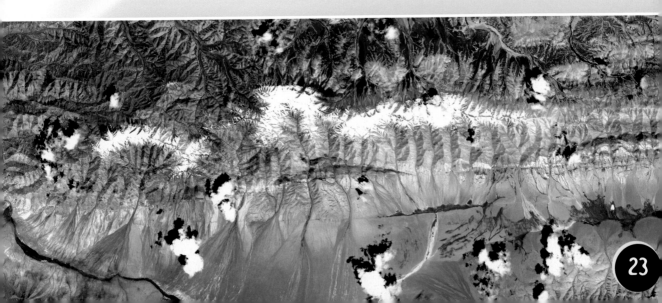

Earth: the Atmosphere

The Earth's atmosphere is a layer of gas that covers the Earth. The atmosphere is vital for life on Earth. It contains gases that plants and animals need to live, it keeps the Earth's surface warm, and it protects life from harmful rays coming from the Sun.

Gases of the atmosphere

Nitrogen makes up 78 per cent of the air, and oxygen makes up 20 per cent. The remainder is made up of many different gases, including carbon dioxide. There is always some water vapour in the atmosphere, too.

The atmosphere is most dense at the Earth's surface. Above the surface the atmosphere becomes thinner and thinner, until it runs out, and space begins, about 100 kilometres up. In the upper atmosphere, there is a special form of oxygen, called ozone, that stops much of the harmful ultraviolet radiation from the Sun from reaching the surface.

Earth Fact

Earth's atmosphere

● An aurora is like a curtain of light in the sky. Auroras are seen near the poles. They happen when particles from the Sun smash into gas in the upper atmosphere, releasing light.

Energetic tropical storms like this form when the air gains heat and water vapour from the warm oceans underneath.

The weather

Winds, clouds and rain all happen in the lowest level of the atmosphere, which is about 10 kilometres thick. The Sun heats some parts of the surface more than others. The surface heats the air above. This makes the air rise and swirl about, causing winds and weather systems. Water from the oceans and the land evaporates into the air, forming water vapour, which is carried along by the wind. When the air cools, the water vapour condenses to form clouds.

The Sun's rays are weak at the poles, and the air never gets warm enough to melt the ice caps.

Climates and seasons

The pattern of weather a place on Earth has is called a climate. Close to the equator, the climate is tropical, with warm, wet weather all year. Close to the poles, the climate is polar, with very cold weather all year. In between, most places have warm summers and cool winters. These seasons happen because Earth's axis is tilted over to one side.

A place has summer when the pole it is nearest to is tilted towards the Sun. On the opposite side of the orbit, this pole is tilted away from the Sun. Then it receives less heat, and it is winter. When it is summer in the northern hemisphere, it is winter in the southern hemisphere, and vice versa. Earth's tilt also means that there are more hours of sunshine in summer than in winter.

A tropical island seen from space. The land is covered with thick vegetation that grows in the warm, rainy climate.

Earth: Water and Life

All animals and plants on Earth are made up of mostly of water. Scientists believe that life can only exist where there is a supply of liquid water. As far as we know, Earth is the only planet or moon in the solar system where there is liquid water, and where there is life.

Earth's water

There is liquid water on Earth because the Earth is just the right distance from the Sun, and because the atmosphere keeps the Earth warm. If the Earth were closer to the Sun, the water would boil away in the heat. If it were further away from the Sun, all the water would be frozen, as it is in the polar ice caps. The region in the Solar System where liquid water can exist on a planet is known as the habitable zone.

Earth's oceans, from warm tropical waters like these to freezing waters near the poles, are teeming with life.

The atmosphere spreads water over the Earth's surface, allowing animals and plants to live on land far from the oceans. Water evaporates from the oceans and moves with the winds.

It condenses to form clouds, and falls onto the surface as rain. This is part of circulation of water between the oceans, atmosphere and land, known as the water cycle.

Scientists think that most of the water on Earth came from volcanoes that erupted soon after the Earth was formed. Some of the water may have come from comets that collided with the Earth.

How do we know?

Remote sensing

We have found out a great deal about the world's water from remote-sensing satellites. The satellites map the temperatures of the oceans, map the seafloor, take photographs of glaciers, and monitor life in the oceans. They send data down to Earth by radio.

How life started

An amazing range of life survives on the Earth, from microscopic plankton in the sea to giant trees on the land. But there was no life when the Earth was formed about 4,600 million years ago. The surface was made of molten rock and there was no water or atmosphere. Hundreds of millions of years later the surface had cooled, but there were still many volcanoes erupting. These brought a mixture of chemicals to the surface. They mixed with pools of water, forming a chemical soup. The chemicals reacted together to form the complex chemicals that are the building blocks of all living things. Eventually, these chemicals came together to make the first, very simple forms of life.

Forms of life, such as these penguins, for example, survive in the most inhospitable regions of the world, from hot, dry deserts to the freezing poles.

Earth's Moon

The Moon is the Earth's only moon. It is about a quarter of the width of the Earth, making it one of the largest moons in the Solar System. Although the Moon is Earth's partner in space, it is a very different place. It is a dry, lifeless world, covered with craters. It looks the same now as it did thousands of millions of years ago.

Orbit and spin

The Moon completes its orbit of the Earth once every 27.3 days. The Moon also spins on its axis just as the Earth does, but very slowly. It completes one spin every time it orbits the Earth. This means that the same side of the Moon faces the Earth all the time. This side is known as the near side. The other side is known as the far side. The far side is always hidden from the Earth.

The near side of the Moon, seen from Earth. The dark patches are known as seas.

Much of our knowledge of the Moon comes from experiments carried out during the Apollo missions.

Craters and seas

The Moon's surface is smothered in craters. Some are a few metres across; others are hundreds of kilometres across. Most craters were formed by meteorites smashing into the Moon in its early life, more than 3,500 million years ago. The craters still exist because there is no erosion on the Moon. The large dark areas on the Moon are known as seas, but they don't contain water. They are giant impact craters that filled with lava that leaked from under the Moon's crust.

Phases and eclipses

The Sun lights up one side of the Moon. As the Moon orbits the Earth, it seems to change shape because we see different amounts of the lit side. A Full Moon is when we see the whole lit side. A New Moon is when we see none of it.

Sometimes the Earth, Moon and Sun are in a perfect straight line. This causes eclipses. A solar eclipse happens when the Moon is directly between the Earth and the Sun. The Moon's shadow falls on the Earth. Anybody in the shadow sees the Sun blocked out by the Moon. A lunar eclipse happens when the Earth is directly between the Sun and Moon. The Earth's shadow falls on the Moon, making it dark.

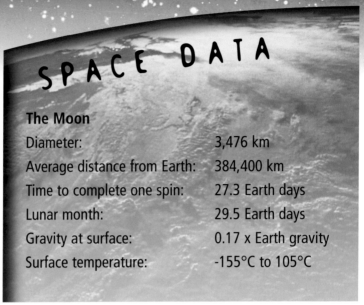

SPACE DATA

The Moon

Diameter:	3,476 km
Average distance from Earth:	384,400 km
Time to complete one spin:	27.3 Earth days
Lunar month:	29.5 Earth days
Gravity at surface:	0.17 x Earth gravity
Surface temperature:	-155°C to 105°C

During a total solar eclipse, gases are visible streaming from the Sun.

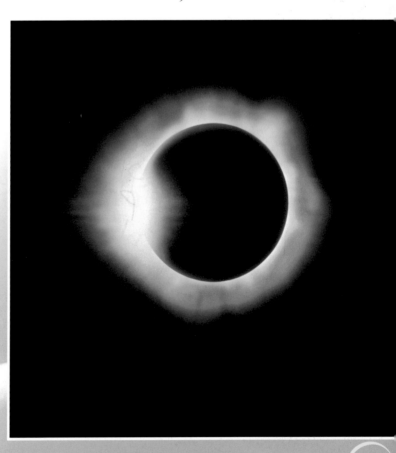

Mars

Mars is the fourth planet from the Sun. Although Mars is only half the size of Earth, and its mass is just one tenth of the mass of Earth, in other ways it is similar to Earth. Mars is known as the 'red planet' because its surface is covered with red-brown rock and dust.

Orbit and spin

Mars is the only rocky planet further from the Sun than the Earth. It takes nearly twice as long as the Earth to complete its orbit. The orbit is quite squashed, so that Mars comes as close as 200 million kilometres to the Sun, and reaches as far as 250 million kilometres from the Sun.

You can clearly see four giant volcanoes on this image of Mars.

The distance between Earth and Mars changes as the planets orbit the Sun. This makes Mars look larger and smaller at different times. It looks largest when it is closest to the Sun in its orbit, and the Earth is on the same side of the Sun as Mars. Then Mars is only about 50 million kilometres away.

Mars spins on its axis at a similar speed to the Earth. It completes one spin every 24.6 Earth hours. Its axis is also tilted over like the Earth's.

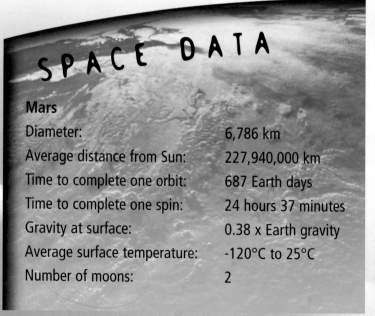

SPACE DATA

Mars

Diameter:	6,786 km
Average distance from Sun:	227,940,000 km
Time to complete one orbit:	687 Earth days
Time to complete one spin:	24 hours 37 minutes
Gravity at surface:	0.38 x Earth gravity
Average surface temperature:	-120°C to 25°C
Number of moons:	2

The atmosphere

Mars has a very thin atmosphere. It is two hundred times thinner than Earth's. More than 95 per cent of the atmosphere is carbon dioxide. The remainder is mainly nitrogen and argon. There is also some water vapour in the atmosphere, which sometimes forms thin clouds.

The Sun heats the surface of Mars, and the surface heats the gas in the atmosphere above. The heating effect is greater near the equator than at the poles, and this causes the gas to swirl about, creating winds. When Mars is at its closest to the Sun, the winds can reach 400 kilometres per hour. Even though the atmosphere is so thin, these strong winds can pick up dust from the surface, forming dust storms. These sometimes cover the whole surface, and take weeks to settle down again.

Internal structure

The internal structure of Mars is similar to the internal structure of the other rocky planets. It has three layers. They are a solid crust on the outside, a thick mantle, and a core. The upper mantle may be slightly molten, because some scientists think that volcanoes on Mars are still spewing out molten rock.

The core of Mars is probably solid. A liquid core would produce a magnetic field, and Mars does not have one.

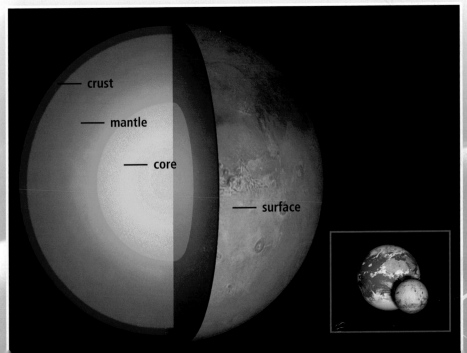

crust

mantle

core

surface

31

Mars: the Surface

The whole surface of Mars is covered with red-brown rocks and dust. There are several dramatic features, such as giant volcanoes and canyons, many times larger than the largest on Earth. The southern hemisphere has much older rocks than the northern hemisphere, and is much rougher, with many craters. The northern hemisphere is smoother, with fewer craters, but many volcanoes.

Giant volcanoes

Near the equator of Mars is an area where the surface bulges out. On top the bulge are three gigantic volcanoes. The largest of the three, called Olympus Mons, is the largest volcano in the whole Solar System. It is 26 kilometres high and 600 kilometres across at the base. These volcanoes are called shield volcanoes because they are very wide, with gentle slopes. They were formed by eruptions of runny lava over billions of years. So far, we haven't seen any of Mars's volcanoes erupting.

Looking straight down onto Olympus Mons. The crater in the middle is about 80 kilometres across.

Canyons and valleys

Mars also features canyons and valleys. These are like dry rivers beds on Earth, and were probably formed by flowing water hundreds of millions of years ago. The largest canyon system is called the Valles Marineris. It stretches about 4,000 kilometres around the equator, and is up to 7 kilometres deep. It may be the remains of giant cracks that formed in the crust.

An impression of the view you would have from inside the giant Valles Marineris canyon on Mars.

Surface temperature

Because Mars is so far from the Sun, and because it has a very thin atmosphere that does not trap heat, its surface is very cold. On average, the temperature is −65°C.

Ice caps

Mars has ice caps at its poles. They are made up of a mixture of water ice (frozen water) and carbon dioxide ice. The ice caps grow in winter as the temperature falls, and water vapour and carbon dioxide from the atmosphere condense and turn solid. They shrink again in summer as the ice turns back to gas.

Space Facts

Mars features

● The volcano Olympus Mons is three times taller than the Earth's tallest volcano, which forms the island of Hawaii.

● The channels on Mars were mistaken for canals by early astronomers. They thought the canals were built by a Martian civilisation.

Mars: Moons

Mars has two moons, called Phobos and Deimos. They are tiny compared to most of the moons in the Solar System. The moons are so hard to spot from Earth that they were not discovered by astronomers until 1877. They are irregular in shape, rather than spherical, like Earth's Moon, and look like giant, dark potatoes.

The moons of Mars, Phobos and Deimos, were discovered in 1877 by Asaph Hall, who named them after characters in Greek mythology.

Captured asteroids

Phobos and Deimos both appear to be asteroids. They were probably captured by the gravity of Mars as they drifted close to the planet. They may have come from the asteroid belt, between the orbits of Mars and Jupiter, where millions of asteroids orbit the Sun. Alternatively, the material that formed the moons may have been left over after the formation of Mars. Both moons orbit much closer to Mars than the Moon orbits Earth. And both spin round on themselves once per orbit, so that the same sides always face Mars.

Both moons are made of very dark rock. Both are also covered in craters, where they have been hit by other asteroids and meteorites. They are covered in a thin layer of dust created by the impacts. Gravity on the moons is extremely weak, but enough to keep the dust in place. Neither moon has an atmosphere.

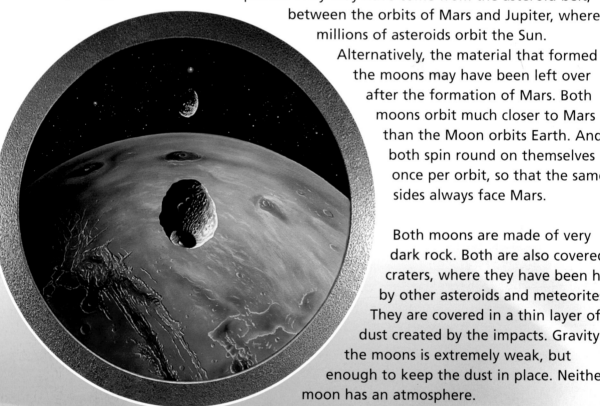

Space Fact

● Phobos is a doomed moon. It is very gradually getting closer to Mars. In about 50 million years time, it will smash into the surface, creating a new crater.

Phobos, the larger moon of Mars. The dip on the left-hand end is a meteorite crater.

Phobos

Phobos is the larger moon, at 28 kilometres long. 'Phobos' is Greek for 'fear'. Phobos is between 18 and 22 kilometres across. At one end of Phobos is a huge crater, 10 kilometres across, which astronomers have named Stickney.

Phobos orbits Mars under 10,000 kilometres from the planet's centre. Because it is so close, it travels at very high speed. It completes a full orbit in just under 8 hours, which is only a third of a Mars day. Seen from Mars, Phobos moves quickly across the sky, in the opposite direction to the Sun and stars.

Deimos

Deimos is even smaller than Phobos, at just 16 kilometres long. It has a smoother, darker surface than Phobos, and fewer craters. It orbits further away from Mars, and more slowly than Phobos, taking about thirty hours to complete an orbit.

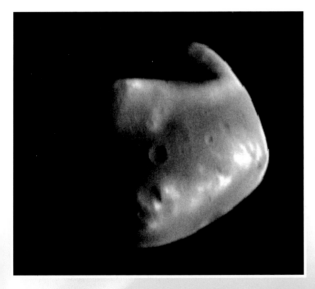

Deimos, the smaller moon of Mars. 'Deimos' is Greek for 'panic'.

Original and enhanced photographs of Phobos and Deimos taken by the Spirit rover.

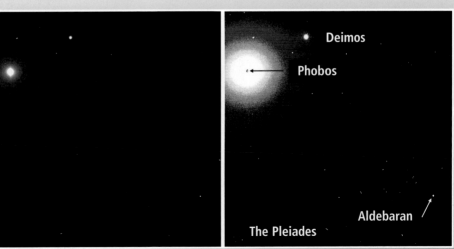

Deimos

Phobos

Aldebaran

The Pleiades

35

Mars: Water and Life

Astronomers think that if there is life anywhere else in the Solar System apart from Earth, then it is probably on Mars. So far we have found no trace of life, but that does not mean there isn't any. And life may have existed in the distant past.

Evidence for water

The forms of life we know on Earth can only exist where there is liquid water. There is water on Mars, but only in the form of gas in the atmosphere or ice on the surface. However, there may be liquid water under the surface. It could be in the form of ice in the soil. There may even be oceans of liquid water under the surface.

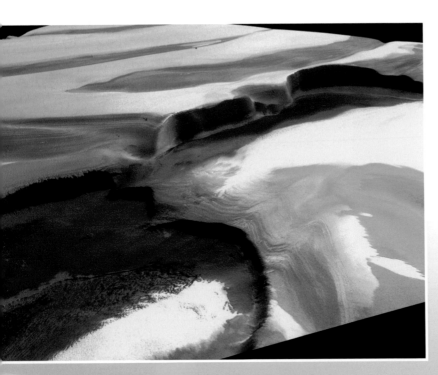

Ice and dust at the north pole of Mars. The ice is a mixture of frozen water and frozen carbon dioxide.

There was almost certainly liquid water on Mars in the past. The numerous channels in the surface could only have been formed by water flowing over thousands or millions of years. There are also flat areas alongside the channels that look like flood plains. Scientists are not sure where Mars's water came from, or where it went.

The search for life

It is impossible for life to exist on the surface of Mars today. There is no liquid water, it is extremely cold, the carbon dioxide in the atmosphere would be poisonous to animals, and the surface is bombarded with powerful and harmful rays from the Sun.

However, if there is liquid water under the surface, there may be life in the form of simple micro-organisms here. After all, simple forms of life survive in extreme places on Earth, such as near hot hydrothermal vents and at the poles.

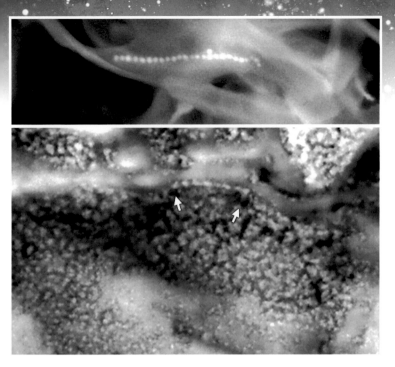

Top: bacteria from Earth. The bright chain is crystals in the bacteria. Bottom: a similar-looking chain in meteorite ALH 84001.

Scientists are not just looking for signs of life on Mars today, but for signs that it existed in the distant past.

Mars fossil

In 1984 a meteorite was found in Antarctica. Analysis of the rock it was made of showed that it could only have come from Mars. It was probably knocked off the planet by a meteorite impact. Inside the meteorite, known as ALH 84001, were tiny rounded lumps that looked like fossil bacteria. There was great excitement at the time, but today scientists think the lumps are tiny rock formations, and not fossils at all.

How do we know?

Mars rovers

Three robot vehicles have driven across the surface of Mars to take photographs and to analyse the rocks and soil. The first was *Sojourner*, in 1997, which was carried to the surface by the Mars *Pathfinder* probe. In 2004, two more rovers, *Spirit* and *Opportunity*, landed on opposite sides of the planet. *Opportunity* found evidence that the rocks had once been under water.

The rover Spirit *on the surface of Mars. Power for the motors and instruments comes from solar cells on top the body.*

How we Observe the Inner Planets

Our knowledge of the Earth and the other inner planets and their moons has come from making careful observations. We observe both from the Earth and from space. We also explore the other planets and moons by sending spacecraft to them. You can find out about exploration on page 40.

Telescopes

The main way of observing the planets (and moons) from Earth is by optical telescope. An optical telescope makes distant objects appear larger. There are two main types of telescope. A refracting telescope uses a lens to collect and focus the light. A reflecting telescope uses a mirror instead. The larger the mirror or lens, the more light that can be collected, and the more detail that can be seen in an object. Most astronomers use reflecting telescopes because they give clearer images. The image made by a telescope's lens or mirror is viewed with an eyepiece, or digitised so that it can be viewed and processed on a computer.

A clearer picture

The air in the Earth's atmosphere swirls about. This makes light from space bend slightly from side to side before it reaches the ground, which is why stars often twinkle at night. This makes it difficult for telescopes on the ground to get a clear picture of the planets. The largest research telescopes use a system called adaptive optics, which changes the shape of the mirror hundreds of times a second to cancel out the distortions caused by the atmosphere.

A hobby telescope like this gives good views of the Moon and planets.

Space telescopes

Space telescopes, such as the Hubble Space Telescope, are telescopes that are up in space. They have two advantages over ground-based telescopes. First, the atmosphere does not distort their images. Secondly, they can detect types of rays that cannot get through the Earth's atmosphere, such as X-rays and ultraviolet rays. Making images of these rays instead of light can tell us more about the planets.

The twin Keck telescopes on the island of Hawaii. Each telescope has a ten-metre wide main mirror.

Remote sensing

It is hard to observe the Earth from the Earth's surface. But we can get a good view from space, from remote-sensing satellites. From their orbits, these satellites can see a wide area of the Earth's surface. They carry a wide variety of sensors, to detect light and other forms of radiation, such as infra-red rays. Remote sensing is used to study the atmosphere, the oceans and the land.

Space facts

Telescope tales

● Large research telescopes are normally situated on mountain tops to give a clearer view of the sky.

● The James Webb Space Telescope (see page 42) will have a 6.5-metre mirror. It will be able to see four hundred times the detail of a similar ground-based telescope.

How we Explore the Inner Planets

Although we can observe the other rocky planets from Earth with telescopes, they are so far away that we can't see much detail. To find out more, we send robot spacecraft called probes, which send back information for us.

Getting into space

Space is only a hundred kilometres away, but it is extremely hard to get there because of the Earth's gravity. A spacecraft must reach 28,000 kilometres per hour to stay in orbit, without falling back to Earth. Spacecraft need an enormous push to lift them into orbit and to reach orbital speed. They need extremely powerful launch vehicles, such as rockets and space shuttles. Their rocket engines produce huge thrust and also work in space, where there is no air. But once in orbit, no engines are needed because there is no air resistance.

An impression of the Phoenix *Mars Lander, which is due to be launched to Mars in 2007.*

Space Facts

- *Mariner 10* was the first probe to use a gravity assist. It used Venus's gravity to slow down so it could reach Mercury.

- Mars *Pathfinder* was the first probe to break its fall with airbags. Its designers got the idea from passenger air bags in cars.

Reaching other planets

Reaching the other planets is as difficult as getting into space in the first place. To escape Earth's gravity completely, and travel into the Solar System, a space probe must travel at about 40,000 kilometres per hour. Probes fly on a curved path (or trajectory) so that they meet a planet in its orbit. The path to the planet must be carefully planned, and the probe must be launched at a certain time if it is to intercept its target planet. The voyages take many months.

A probe often flies close to another planet on the way to its target planet. It uses the gravity of the planet to speed up, slow down or change direction. This is called a gravity assist, and it means the probe can carry much less fuel.

Orbiting and landing

Most probes go into orbit around another planet. Others are designed to land on the planet, or carry separate landers that they release to descend to the surface. Landers slow their descent with parachutes, or break their fall with air bags.

Anatomy of a probe

The main parts of a probe are its propulsion unit, a communications aerial, sensors that gather information, and a power source for its electronic circuits. The aerial detects radio signals from Earth that control the probe, and sends data signals back to Earth. Power comes from solar arrays or small nuclear power plants.

A Russian Soyuz-FG-Fregat launcher lifts off, carrying the Venus Express *probe into space.*

41

The Future

What is left to find out about the inner planets, and how will we observe them and explore them in the future? And what will happen to the inner planets, including the Earth, in the distant future?

In 2004, American President George W. Bush announced that a new manned space program would visit the Moon and Mars.

Future probes and observations

Several new space probe missions to the inner planets are planned. Probes will orbit the planets, mapping them in great detail, and probes will land to study their atmospheres, rocks, and to search for water and signs of life. New missions are also planned to find out more about the Moon.

More powerful telescopes, both on the ground and in space, will add to our knowledge of the planets. The replacement for the aging Hubble Space Telescope, called the James Webb Space Telescope, will give much clearer views of the planets after its launch which is scheduled for 2013.

Space Fact

● Following its launch, the James Webb Space Telescope will be sent into orbit 1.5 million km from the Earth. It will have a mirror measuring 6.5 m across and have a sunshield as big as a tennis court.

Man to Mars

The American space agency NASA is developing the successor to the space shuttle, called the Crew Exploration Vehicle. This will be launched by rocket. They plan to send astronauts to the Moon by 2020. They will explore the Moon, but also use the missions to test the technology for a manned mission to Mars. But years of work are needed to make sure their journey will be a safe one.

Perhaps we should try to reduce carbon emissions before spending fortunes on exploring the Solar System.

Earth's problems

Many scientists say that we should be solving problems on Earth before spending our resources to explore the other planets. The greatest issue is that of global warming and climate change, which need to be halted and reversed before they cause major problems for us. Other scientists argue that exploring will provide us with knowledge about how our own world works, and how it could change in the future.

Long term changes

Over millions of years, the Earth's surface will continue to change, with new mountain ranges forming and being eroded away again, and the continents drifting across the surface. Perhaps in the distant future it will look like Mars does today. The surfaces of Venus and Mars will change, too, as volcanoes continue to erupt. But Mercury will stay as it is today, a dead, unchanging world.

In about 5,000 million years time the Sun will run out of fuel. Then it will grow into a red ball of hot gas, so large that it will swallow up all the inner planets. They will all be destroyed.

Timeline of Discovery

1609   Astronomer Thomas Harriot uses a telescope to draw the first accurate map of the Moon.

1666   Giovanni Cassini discovers the Martian ice caps.

1877   Asaph Hall discovers the moons of Mars.

1959   *Luna 1* is the first probe to fly past the Moon.

1959   *Luna 3* is the first probe to see the far side of the Moon.

1962   *Mariner 2* is the first probe to fly past Venus.

1964   The first *Nimbus* remote-sensing satellite is launched for studying the oceans and atmosphere.

1965   *Mariner 4* is the first probe to photograph Mars after being launched the previous year.

1966   *Luna 9* is the first probe to make a successful landing on the Moon.

1969   Astronauts land on the Moon for the first time aboard *Apollo 11*.

1970   The first lunar rover, *Lunokhod 1*, lands on the Moon.

The probe Mariner 2, *the first probe to visit Venus.*

1970	*Venera 7* reaches the surface of Venus, the first probe to survive on the surface and send data back to Earth.
1972	The first Landsat satellite, *ERTS 1*, is launched to photograph and study the Earth's surface.
1974	*Mariner 10* flies past Mercury, taking photographs of the planet.
1975	*Venera 9* sends back the first photographs of the surface of Venus.
1989	The *Magellan* probe is launched and the following year maps the surface of Venus using radar.
1996	Mars *Global Surveyor* is launched. In 1997 it enters Mars's orbit and maps the surface of the planet.
1997	Mars *Pathfinder* lands on Mars after its launch the previous year. It carries a robot vehicle, called *Sojourner*, that drives slowly across the surface.
1998	*Lunar Prospector* orbits the Moon, and finds evidence of water ice in craters.
2006	*Venus Express* arrives in orbit around Venus.

The view of Mars from the Pathfinder *probe. The* Sojourner *rover is investigating the large, central rock.*

Glossary

asteroid A rocky object that orbits the Sun, but that is not large enough to be a planet. Most asteroids orbit between the orbits of Mars and Jupiter.

astronomer A scientist who studies planets, moons and other objects in space.

atmosphere A layer of gas that surrounds a planet or moon.

atmospheric pressure The push from the air on objects in the atmosphere.

comet A small, icy object that orbits the Sun.

condense To turn from gas to liquid.

continent A large land mass on the Earth (there are currently seven continents).

crater A dish-shaped hole in the surface of a planet or moon, created by an object from space smashing into the surface.

crust The solid, outer layer of the Earth.

erosion The gradual wearing away of the landscape by the weather and flowing water.

evaporate To turn from liquid to gas.

glacier A river of ice that flows slowly down from an ice-covered mountain range.

gravity A force that attracts all objects to each other.

hydrothermal vent A place on the ocean floor where hot water emerges from rocks underneath.

lava The name for molten rock after it comes from a volcano.

lunar To do with the Moon.

meteorite A rocky particle from space that crashes into the surface of a planet or moon.

moon An object that orbits around a planet, but that is not part of a planet's rings.

nebula A giant cloud of gas and dust in space.

nuclear reaction When the nucleus of an atom splits apart, or loses or gains some particles.

orbit 1) Moving around the Sun or a planet; 2) The path that an object takes as it moves around the Sun or a planet.

ozone A gas that is a special form of oxygen (each particle is made up of three oxygen atoms instead of the normal two).

planet An object in space that orbits around the Sun, but that is not part of a large group of objects, such as asteroids or comets.

probe A spacecraft sent into space to send back information about the Sun, other planets or moons.

satellite A spacecraft that orbits around the Earth.

solar array A panel of solar cells that turn sunlight into electricity.

tectonic plate One of the giant pieces that the Earth's crust is broken into.

water vapour The gas form of water, made when liquid water boils.

Further Information

Books

Mars (True Books)
Elaine London, Children's Press, 2008

National Geographic Encyclopedia of Space
Linda K. Glover
National Geographic Society, 2005

Organizations

National Aeronautics & Space
Administration (NASA)
Organization that runs the US
space program
www.nasa.gov

International Astronomical Union (IAU)
The official world astronomy organization,
responsible for naming star, planets, moons
and other objects in space
www.iau.org

Jet Propulsion Laboratory (JPL)
Centre responsible for NASA's robot
space probes
www.jpl.nasa.gov

European Space Agency (ESA)
Organization responsible for space flight
and exploration of European countries
www.esa.int

The Planetary Society
Organization devoted to the exploration of
the Solar System
www.planetary.org

Websites

http://nssdc.gsfc.nasa.gov/planetary/
factsheet/
All the facts and figures you could ever
need about the inner planets

www.nineplanets.org
Lots of information about the planets

http://sse.jpl.nasa.gov/kids/index.cfm
NASA pages for children about exploring
the Solar System

http://dsc.discovery.com/guides/planetearth/
planetearth.html
Discovery Channel site about the Earth,
with interesting videos

http://mars.jpl.nasa.gov/funzone_flash.html
Fun activities all to with Mars

http://www.keckobservatory.org/
All about the Keck telescopes in Hawaii

Index

Numbers in **bold** indicate pictures.